Divorce by Deployment

Divorce by Deployment

◆

My story, My tragedy, My victory

Percell Artis Jr.

iUniverse, Inc.
New York Lincoln Shanghai

Divorce by Deployment
My story, My tragedy, My victory

Copyright © 2006 by Percell Artis Jr.

iUniverse books may be ordered through booksellers or by contacting:

iUniverse
2021 Pine Lake Road, Suite 100
Lincoln, NE 68512
www.iuniverse.com
1-800-Authors (1-800-288-4677)

The views expressed in this work are solely those of the author and do not necessarily reflect the views of the publisher, and the publisher hereby disclaims any responsibility for them.

ISBN-13: 978-0-595-41609-7 (pbk)
ISBN-13: 978-0-595-85958-0 (ebk)
ISBN-10: 0-595-41609-8 (pbk)
ISBN-10: 0-595-85958-5 (ebk)

Printed in the United States of America

In memory of my mother and father.

Contents

Acknowledgments

Thank you Lord for my parents especially my mother! She took care of me for 44 years. I love you and miss you greatly. She instilled in me the very thing that I believe in today which is:

Love and trust God.

Always, always tell the truth.

Be honest.

Treat people like you want them to treat you.

Don't hurt no one's feelings.

If you get angry, walk away.

Thank you Lord for my maternal side of the family: My aunts: Ester and Virginia. My fantastic cousins: Francis, Linda, Barbara, Emily, Kiffaney and Robin. I love you all so much!

Thank you Lord for my paternal side of the family. My uncles: Earl, Douglas and Roger (RW). My aunts: Juanita, Cleo, Elnora. My cousins: Ernest, Willie, Larry and Glory. If I forgot to mention anyone, please forgive me. I love you all!

Thank you Lord for giving me great friends! Way too many to mention!

To 'Levern'. I love you! I can't say it enough. You have been unbelievable! You have supported me in everything I have done. I can't remember how many times I have been away from you, especially with the many deployments, but you have never let me down!

You have raised, taught, inspired and treated the Bo like he was your very own child. Thank you for showing me how to open up, laugh and enjoy life. I thank you for sticking with me through thick and thin. I enjoy our evening walks. Again, I love you!

To my daughter and the Bo, I hope you are proud to have me as your father, as I am proud to have you as my children! I love you both!

To my schools:

Crestwood Elementary and Junior High School.	The beginning.
Great Bridge High School (Class of '80).	The middle.
Norfolk State University (Class of '84). B.S. Mass Communications.	I hope not the end!

To my neighborhood of Crest Harbor, I miss the old times!

To my fraternity: Alpha Phi Alpha. Recognized as the first established inter-collegiate service fraterinity for African Americans, founded in 1906, I am so proud to be a member. Happy 100th! "First of all, Servants of all, We transcend all!"

To my many military friends: There is no way that I can mention all of your names, but to everyone I have served with, I cherish the times that we spent together. I honor you. Thanks for serving your country!

A big thanks to my publisher, iUniverse and my Publishing Services Associate, Rachele Walter!

To my personal editors: 'Levern', LTC Creal, SFC King-Johns, MSgt 'Big Daddy James' (congrats on the PT test!) and many others that inspired me to get the word out, thanks!

A special thanks to SGM Stuart: I wanted to quit, but you kept me going! You taught me to visualize the entire picture when I write. You have made me better writer.

Think you may know me? The following lists are places I have been stationed.

Three separate tours of Germany: Linderhoffe, Schwabisch Hall, Hanau and Stuttgart. I also had a tour of Korea.

My stateside assignments have been: Ft. Jackson, SC, Vint Hill Farms, VA, Ft. Knox, KY, Virginia Military Institute (VMI), Ft Lewis, WA and Mac Dill AFB FL.

I have been deployed to the following countries: Kosovo, Macedonia, Greece, Albania, Bosnia, Afghanistan, Africa and two tours to Qatar.

I truly appreciate your support! Thank you! Thank you all!

Last but not least, I would like to thank **me**! I have never worked so hard in my life getting this book completed!

Peace!!!

Percell

Preface

The title of this book, *Divorce by Deployment,* revolves around my legal separation, while I was deployed to Kosovo and subsequent divorce. This is a personal story of my first wife, our son, her men, her pregnancy, the US Army, and me while I was deployed. I hope to give an optimistic view and insight as to how the end of this marriage affected my life.

This book looks at how I dealt with several tragic events during that time. I'm not suggesting that my story is the worst event man has ever lived; but it was catastrophic to me. With all that my first wife put me through, I could have easily done something stupid that would have ruined my life forever.

Thank goodness, I woke up and smelled the coffee before it was too late. I know from my own personal experiences that no matter how bad you feel about yourself or your situation, there is always someone or something out there that is willing to help guide you down the right path. For me, I chose to write.

Allow me to briefly introduce myself and give you my family background. My name is Percell Artis Jr., the only child of Percell Sr. and Lucille Artis. My parents called me Junior. I am an African American, about five-foot seven inches tall, medium built and by all standards an average looking guy. I was born in 1962 and raised in Chesapeake, Virginia.

My father's side of the family is rather large and scattered up and down the east coast. My grandfather married twice and my father, along with his brother, were the only kids from his first marriage. My grandfather's second wife had many children, who I did not meet for the first time until I was eight years old. Unfortunately, because of the distance I never really got to know them very well.

I was closer to my mother's side of the family and spent quality time with them daily. She had six brothers and sisters who all lived with their families in Chesapeake. I am the only boy on my mothers' side of the family and was very close to my cousins. Sunday was the big family day. Almost every week we all gathered for Sunday dinner at the home of one of her sisters.

My parents (as you will read later in the book) had lots of marital problems. As far as I know, he never cheated on her but the normal routine was for my father to get drunk and start a fight with my mom about petty stuff. Too often, I found myself caught in the middle of all the drama.

His many bouts were referred to as 'getting drunk' or 'Percell got his head bad last night'. I never heard anyone refer to him as what he was, an alcoholic in denial. Thanks to my father's actions, I have never consumed alcohol nor smoked in my life.

Despite his abuse, my mother stayed with my father until the day he died. Divorce was out of the question and never referred to. Marriage counseling was simply not an option. Her idea of 'marriage counseling' was to storm out in anger and stay overnight with one of her sisters. She would always return home to my father and I the next day.

She would later tell me after he died, that she loved my father, but did not love the way he treated her. It was important to her to stick it out because she did not want me to grow up like my father, who came from a broken home.

Her belief was instilled in me, and years later I realized that I too was holding on to my failed marriage for the exact same reasons. I did not believe in divorce and found myself in mental anguish as I tried to keep my son under the same roof with his mother and me.

I thought that I had done all the right things. One of my main goals was to never be like my father. I married at the ripe age of twenty-eight. I thought I had a good wife. She was not perfect and neither was I, but initially we respected each other.

Our marriage was going great for the first few years. Somehow, communication started to break down and by our eighth year, things were looking bleak.

It was a rainy night in Kosovo. I think I was in my second month there, when I realized that my marriage was forever broken. I was so distraught, that I did something that was unusual for me; I started to write.

I also wrote about Kosovo. Night after night I found refuge writing not only about the people I had met, but my day-to-day experiences and my failed marriage.

Also included in this book are details about:

- My father who was truly a difficult person. He rarely showed my mother and I any affection. Find out about how his outrageous past crept into my life and ultimately affected my marriage.

- How my wife and I only had unprotected sex once, but she ended up with two kids by two different 'baby daddies' *after* we were married.

- My love and respect for the Albanian people. They helped expose me to a different outlook on life.

- The love of one person who truly picked me up when I was at my lowest point.
- The weekly radio program that I started in Kosovo! The people of Kosovo took my radio program to another level and showed me love!

I hope you will enjoy reading *Divorce by Deployment*.

1

Back in the day

Since I have stated my views on divorce, I guess I can look at my upbringing on that topic. I did not come from a 'model' family. My father was one mean SOB. He treated my mom (and sometimes me) like crap. Ever so often, he was ok. But it was too seldom. There was a few times I even saw a comedic side of him. You will read about that later. He was a bit complicated and very hard to figure out.

As the old saying goes, there are two sides to every story and I tried to understand his. My father (who was born in 1926) was the eldest of two boys. After dad's youngest brother Roger William (RW for short) was born, my grandfather left his family and never returned. During the great depression, times were especially tough on my father's family. With one source of money barley coming in, my grandmother made a decision. In 1941, she made my father drop out of school at the age of 15 to work and support the family.

Late in his life he would tell me that she was really hard to please. She never made RW quit school, nor work when he was out of school in the summer. He told me that he always resented the difference in treatment. He said that she would yell at him most of the time when things went wrong and that is probably why his father left. She was never pleased with anything.

My earliest remembrance of my grandmother was in 1972 when I was 10 years old. She was in her mid 70's at the time. Boy! Did she look mean! She had that classic grandmother look. Her hair was kind of blue-gray. She had a small scraggly mustache. She wore those old timers' eyeglasses. She had some hair under her chin and she dipped and spit snuff. She had big cheeks that were soft but always smelled like rubbing alcohol. So, as a kid, seeing how she looked and smelled, I was afraid of her. Not because she was mean or treated me unkindly, I remembered how she treated my father.

I never liked going to her house, because it always smelled musty. She kept her rooms dimly lit. It was always hard to see. When you walked, the floors creaked and in some widows, spider webs grew. I truly thought that her place was haunted. When she saw me she would always say, "Come here baby and give your grandmother a big kiss". I had to kiss those big old cheeks of hers. I always cried at that point.

When I was a young child, my father dropped me off at my grandmother's house in Portsmouth, Virginia. As my kid mentality worked, I used to think of this as some type of punishment. When my father would leave, I would look out the window at his car as if to say 'don't leave me here'. My grandmother loved it when I came over. She would always take me to the corner store. She would go into her room and get dressed. It would take forever for her to come out. That meant I had to sit there practically in the dark. Wide eyed, I just knew something would jump out and attack me!

When we walked to the store, she would hold my hand tightly. By doing this, our hands would start to sweat. Yuck! She stopped just about everyone along the way to tell people that I was her grandchild. A ten-minute walk to the store ended up being a half an hour walk. She was proud of me.

When we got to the store, I'd wiped my hand on my shirt. She always got on me for that. While in the store she would buy 'Goodies' powder. That was the snuff that she dipped with. For me, she purchased nickel candy. That was a lot of candy for five cents back in the day. While standing in the check out line, she would get so impatient, fussing and cussing at how slow the line was moving. I was reminded that my father acted the same way when we were in a line.

I mentioned earlier, she never mistreated me. She always loved me being around her. My father and his brother, RW, would always check on her. When the two brothers were there at the same time, it was very quiet. The only noise you would hear is from her old AM radio. There wasn't much talking. It was one of the few times I've seen my father humbled by her. He acted like a child himself, sitting there as if he was afraid to say anything. Sometimes he would keep his head down, as if he was afraid to make eye contact with her. When her children said something she did not like, she would speak to RW civilly; however, if it was my father who made the comment, she'd rip into him. I sensed that RW was her favorite.

Overall, I think she loved both of them equally. She was proud of them. Both had served in the Korean War while my father served in the navy and RW was in the army. Later on, my father had become one of the top black electricians in Virginia. He was good with his hands and she called my father often to fix things around her house.

Because her house was so old, my grandmother's calls added up quickly. She only called on RW to run errands. Again, it seemed to my dad, RW would get off easy. When she died a few years later, it was the first and only time I saw my father cry.

So, I had him figured out. He acted like a bad ass when nobody was around. He talked to my mom and showed her no respect. When his friends were around us he treated us like humans.

I knew deep in my heart he loved us, but had a difficult time showing it. I think he really wanted to act in another way, but did not know how. He was forced to draw from what he was used to; the verbal abuse that his mother gave him. I am not defending him; I'm just trying to tell both sides of his story from what I saw and what he has told me.

The last few years of my fathers' life he told me it was just RW and he. His mother was under a lot of pressure to keep the boys in line and often took out her aggression on him.

As a young boy, I kept my room door closed. I always did this because my father would yell at my mother most of the time. Out of 7 days in a week, he was fussing and cussing at least 5 of those days. He was never pleased with anything.

My mother was a teacher for over 20 years and worked with special needs kids. She retired in 1984, the year I graduated from college. She was also the home-maker and kept the house very clean. She cooked great meals and tried everything she could in making my father happy. My father and reluctant mother started a small business out of our house. It was called P & L Electric Company. My mom kept the records of the business and wrote the checks. I guess you can say that she was the bookkeeper.

My father had plenty of work and was very well known throughout the area for his abilities as an electrician. He never left a job unfinished and always worked late. (You will see why in a minute). I used to go with him on the weekends to watch and 'learn' the business. I never like the idea of getting shocked to make a living.

He could tell that I wasn't very interested in the business. One day, he was so pissed at me that he said that I would not amount to anything. From that moment on, I was driven to make him eat those words. "One day, I will show him that I will be somebody," I said to myself.

My father hired a couple of men to work for him. One of the men my father hired was my uncle named (believe it or not) Toyie. Uncle Toyie was very slow at everything he did. He always had a cigarette in his mouth and coughed a lot. Uncle Toyie often worked so slow that my father had to take over and do his job. I remembered one time Uncle Toyie had wired someone's light fixture way off center. My father put him on another job in the house. Ten minutes later my uncle rewired a light switch so badly that when you touched it you would get shocked!

The other guy my father hired was a guy named 'Man'. I never knew his real name. 'Man' was pretty good at what he did. The only problem was that 'Man' smoked a lot of weed. That would cause 'Man' to be late some days.

When my father came home from work grumpy, something had always gone wrong. One day 'Man' was really late for work. I think my dad had to go to his house. He found 'Man' half nude and unable to work. Instead of firing him he 'fired off' on my mom and me, as if it was our fault.

After owning the business for a few years, the pressure was catching up on him and he did not want to let it go. I'll give him credit. He stuck with it for long as he could, and as I said before he worked a lot of late hours by himself.

Meet my father; the big shot

I don't want to paint a bad picture of my father. He also did some funny stuff. I guess I could say that he was a 'trip'. I would like to share a few of these stories with you.

My dad was a good provider; he had plenty of money and always bought us gifts. We had somewhat of a fancy house. He rewired much of it with fancy lighting fixtures. He never had us 'wanting' for material things. All we really wanted was his love.

One side of me was so proud of him. He was a big shot to me. He was well respected in our community and quite popular. I never saw him without a pocket full of money. I remember one day he told me that he was going to buy a TV. He asked me if I wanted to go. I didn't see the big deal so I told him no. This was one of the few times he did not make me go with him. I guess he was reaching out to me, but I knew how he acted in public for his impatience so I decided to stay home.

Two hours later, I heard a van blow its horn. It was my fathers' work van. He rolled down the window and yelled for me to come out. He was making so much noise that everyone on our block came outside to see what was going on. I guess some people thought my parents had gotten into another knock down, drag out fight. He opened the door and there was a 28 inch Zenith TV in a box. That was a huge TV back in the day. It took my father and our next-door neighbor along with me to unload it from the van. We were the first in our block to have a TV that big.

He was so proud of it. He purposely opened the big box on our lawn so everyone could see it. Then he got a lawn chair and sat down and read the instructions underneath a sun umbrella. Some of our friends came over to look at it. He stood there as if he was holding an interview session, fielding questions about the TV. This was no ordinary television; it was cut in a half circle and could fit in a corner of any room. You could hook up a phone line to it and with the 'new' brick remote control, not only change channels without getting up but also answer the phone through the TV!

You may think that this TV was really great back in the day. Well it was, but it had a one major drawn back. It did not have an antenna. Some people that were born after 1985 may not know what I am talking about. Today's TV's are easy; buy it, un box it, plug it into the wall, screw the cable in the back of the TV and the other end in the wall. There you have it, a nice color TV with a great picture.

Our TV 'cable' ran up a tall pole, and was attached to the antenna that was on our roof. I cannot tell you how many times I got on the roof and moved the antenna to get a 'clear' picture. It did not matter if it was raining or not!

That same TV almost got me fired from my first job. I used to work part time at a radio station. You will read about that in another chapter. Anyway, the station had a big contest. We were giving away free concert tickets to one of the hottest singers during this time, Luther Vandross. When news spread that he was indeed coming to our area, the tickets sold out fast. The local concert promoter gave us 20 pairs of tickets and one pair of backstage passes for our listeners.

We had been giving away tickets for almost a week. We promoted the grand prize giveaway was not only free tickets to the show, but a free dinner before the concert. We also threw in a limousine ride to and from the show, and the backstage passes!

The station manger decided to give *me* the opportunity on my show to host the grand prize finale. The station promoted this big event for almost two weeks. My job was to simply announce that the contest was ready to start and the winner would be the 20th caller at the station's 'hot line' phone.

That day that the radio station was buzzing with excitement, many people were calling in before the time that I was supposed to give the grand prize away. This was a big deal to many people to have a chance to meet Luther. I was nervous, because I knew that many listeners were out there and I did not want anything to go wrong.

The time came for me to make the big announcement. I said, "It is time for the grand prize finale. Please be the 20th caller and not only will you win tickets to see Luther Vandross, but you will ride to the concert in style in our own limo. We will take you and your guest to dinner and after the show, you will meet Luther himself. Call now and be lucky number 20!"

The phones were ringing off the hook. I heard 19 disappointed voices. Especially number 19, she was crying and yelling that she missed only by one phone call.

Now it was time for number twenty. I faded the music down and with our pre recorded drum roll, I said, "Here is lucky number twenty!!" Tell me your name!!"

A muffled voice came over the radio. At first it sounded a little distorted. "Hello," the man's voice said. It sounded like he was talking through a can. I thought that he was listening to the radio and talking to me at the same time.

"Hello?" I said, "Please turn down your radio. What is your name and where are you calling from?"

"Hello? Junior? It's me, your father. I have RW with me and we are talking to you through the TV. How do we sound?"

I was in shock! My father called during the most important radio contest we have had!

Before I could say anything else he said, "Hold on, let me get your mother in here so she can talk to you. 'Hey Lucille!!! Come in here I have Junior on the phone."

Then RW said, "Hey Junior. How do we sound?"

I quickly (but not quickly enough) turned on some music, faded them off the radio and made up an excuse that we are having 'technical difficulties.'

My station manger was not pleased.

The last story about my father that I would like to share with you is how his anger got the best of him. This time, my mom and I and some of our neighbors were on the laughing end of this event.

One day my father talked my mom and me into going to Sears with him. My mom's car was a red 1969 Ford Mustang. This is the first car that I remember as a child. I can't remember if my parents bought the car new or used. It must have been used. I remember blue smoke coming from the tail pipe every time she drove off.

After a while, her car started giving her problems. One time it did not start. Another time when she started it, the car backfired so loudly that a few neighbors thought my father was shooting a gun. She said she would never start that car again.

So, unbeknownst to my father, my mother borrowed her sister's car to drive to and from work. Some days her sister picked her up at our house and dropped her off at work. On those days she caught a ride home with someone that was coming in the direction of our house.

My mom was afraid to ask my father to purchase a new car. After all, he worked all the time and was in a bad mood most of the time.

This particular day however, he wanted to drive the Mustang into town and roll down the windows and show it off. She tried to tell him not to drive the car. As usual, he started yelling. My mother suggested that he drive the work van instead.

As he thought about his answer, he looked at the front yard. It was trash day and he did not see our trashcan where it was supposed to be. Then he started yelling at me for not taking out the trash. I went to the back yard where we kept this big, green stinky trashcan, which was filled to the top.

My mom had just bought us some new pillows for us so she threw out the old feathered ones. They were stuffed at the top. I pushed the pillows down into the can and close the top.

As I was dragging the heavy trashcan to its usual place out front, my parents were in my mother's car. My mother opened the door for me; she got out and leaned the front seat towards her so I could get in.

Once we were all in the car, my mother said, "Please be careful." My father had a puzzled look on his face. He pumped the gas pedal and started the car.

'Click, Click, Vroom. Bang!

The car shuddered at bit. Then it was silence.

"Do you smell anything?" my mother said. "Be quiet. I know what I am doing." as my father tried to start the car.

"Hey, I smell it too!" I shouted. By this time my father thought that we did not want to go to Sears. He yelled, "We are going to the store now shut up!'

All of a sudden he opened the door of the car. We quickly jumped out. He went to the front of the car. "Oh, this is nothing. I don't know why y'all are so scared. I can fix any car. You must have forgotten to put oil or water in the car. Junior, bring me that trashcan over here. I will check the oil gage and I need some old paper to wipe off the oil stick," he said proudly.

I drugged the trashcan right next to him. He opened the car's hood.

Whoosh!!!!!

The car's engine was on fire and there was smoke everywhere!

Without looking, he opened the trashcan and grabbed the first thing he put his hands on. It was one of those old feather pillows. By this time some of our neighbors were outside to see where all of the smoke was coming from. One yelled out to my mother that she had called the fire department.

Meanwhile, my father was beating the engine to death with the feathered pillow. There was smoke and feathers everywhere. When the fire department came, my father's white shirt was gray and he had an Afro full of feathers!

Everyone was chuckling at my father, even the firemen.

The next day my father purchased a new green 1974 Ford LTD for my mother.

Inside our house we also had the first VCR on our block. I guess it cost somewhere over $500. We had a citizen band radio with a police scanner and the highest citizen band radio antenna in the community. We had an eight-track machine, a reel-to-reel, and a component system with huge speakers that he hung on the walls. I guess you can say we had the first 'surround sound' system in our neighborhood. I still have in my possession his Magnavox speakers. This led to my pleasure in music that I still have today.

Our house had wall-to-wall carpeting and an intercom system that ran to every room in the house and outside in our back yard. The system had an am/fm radio combination. When we had guests, he would turn on the intercom to his favorite station.

During the summer he bought a riding lawn mower for our small yard and a gas grill. He also equipped our house with the first security system in our community that had two loud ass horns up in both corners of our house. I was so embarrassed with that alarm system and kids teased me about it.

When he first tested the system, a couple of neighbors called the police on us for disturbing the peace! If the wind blew hard enough, it would set off the alarm. That damn thing used to go off in the middle of the night and would scare the crap out of me.

One day I was riding home on the school bus and our alarm was going off. The kids laughed at me and told me to hurry up and catch the robber. Six months later he disconnected it.

He also tinkered with electronic trains. We had a model train set that took up half of our family room. We had a built in bar where he drank most of the time and listen to old school music.

As a hobby, he played pool and could beat anyone on the checkerboard.

My father knew his limit of spending. I was so amazed at how he spent and gave away money and was never broke. He taught me how to save money and to this day, I keep a certain amount in my account.

I remember asking him for $10 one day. He barked at me and asked when I was going to pay it back. Hell, I was only ten at the time and did not have a part time job! He interrogated me so much; he brought tears in my eyes. He told me, "Stop crying; that's for women."

With that experience, I found out how he got back some of the money he lent people. He would ask so many questions about when or how he would get the money back; he made you feel guilty about asking for it in the first place.

Ass kicking days

Still, money can't buy happiness. We were never a happy family. We could all be watching the same TV program but in three different rooms. When my father was drunk, 'watch out'! Fists were going to fly that night. One night my father pushed my mother down and was standing over her as if to hit her again. I ran in the room to break it up and he pushed me as well. I got up and looked at him. He gave me a look as if to say, 'try it'.

A day that I will never forget is the day my father 'lost his mind' in the house. My mother had just finished some small housework and my father started fussing as usual about the business and the checks not being done. My mother (who use to call him 'Pert' for short) yelled back at him and said, "Pert, I am tired and I don't feel like arguing with you!" To him, the comment was disrespectful. "Don't talk back to me!" he said. Then there was silence.

As I opened my door to look in the hallway, I saw my father walk quickly to their bedroom as if he was looking for something. I ran to the room to try to calm him down. He was throwing clothes around in the room. I thought to myself he must be looking for a gun. He didn't find what he was looking for. He pushed me aside as he walked back to my mother. I grabbed his shirttail. He said, "Get your hands off of me. Don't ever put your hands on me," as he pushed me on the floor. I think my mother jumped on his back. As I stood up they were in some type of turning and twisting motion.

I was so afraid I ran to my aunt's house (she lived four houses from us). I told her that my father was going to kill my mom. She and my uncle Toyie (who called the police) went to my house. "Stay here, we will get him", my aunt told me. A half an hour later, my aunt called and told me to come home and everything was ok.

That night for the rest of their lives, my mother slept in a separate room.

This was one of two times I remember leaving the house that way. The other time my father was yelling loudly at my mother and I could not take it any longer. I jumped in my car and drove to my girlfriend's house. When I arrived, I was crying. I told my girlfriend's mother what happened and she called home to see if everything was ok. I was relived when she informed me that my Mom was ok and that my father left the house.

I was 17 at the time; but cried like a baby. It seemed everyone in my neighborhood knew our problems. Had I been older, I would have kicked my father's ass. Then I would kick it again for good measure.

He should have never treated her that way nor laid a hand on her. The mental and physical anguish he put her through was unnecessary. His treatment of her affected her until the day she died.

Because of that I will never forget nor forgive him.

My mother stayed with him over 30 years because of me. She did not want me to grow up without a father, no matter how bad he was at times. This was the time of the '70's and divorce was unusual where we were from. At my young age, I can honestly say to you that I never, ever heard the word divorce. Marriage counseling was definitely Greek to us. That stuff was for the 'white folks'. I knew it crossed her mind to leave him many times but she hung in there for me. With every ass kicking she took, she took it for me. Mom, I will always love you for that!

2

At the Club

I joined the army in 1986. After basic training, I was stationed in northern Virginia. I was there only a year and was reassigned in June 1987 to a tiny northern city called Linderhofe, Germany.

I met my wife in late 1987. Like many servicemen stationed abroad, we met in a nightclub. When I first saw her, she was sitting at the bar talking to one of her friends. She had striking bleached blonde hair and deep blue eyes. At first glance, she reminded me of a young Marilyn Monroe.

Her English was surprisingly good the first time we talked. She tried to teach me some small words in German. I asked her to dance, so I could get to know her better. We danced many times that night.

We met regularly at the club on Friday nights. After a few weeks I noticed like clockwork that the DJ would start to play dance music at 10:30 p.m. It was during that time we met on the dance floor.

After a few weeks of seeing her without a date, I finally gathered enough nerve to ask her whether she had a boyfriend. Just as I was about to poise the question, a guy interrupted us and asked her to dance. After the dance, her girlfriend immediately started speaking to her in German.

When the DJ played a slow song, I saw my chance and asked her to dance. I slid over to her took her hand and led her onto the dance floor.

"Do you have a boyfriend?" I squeaked.

"What?" She said. "Please speak a littler slower"

"Are you seeing someone special?" I stuttered.

"Oh, I see. No. Not at this time. I have a friend but he is in the army." She said.

"Oh", I whispered.

I was crushed. I did not want her to see my face. I imagined that at any time some big army dude would come in the club and find us slow dancing. I did not say anything for a while. I was looking around the club for any potential trouble. As I was slowly backing away from her, the silence was broken.

"He is in the German army. He is in the southern part of Germany. He will be there for nine months." She said.

I breathed a sigh of relief as a big smile came across my face. At least for now, she was mine.

"Would you mind showing me some of the castles that are here? Everything is in German and you could interpret for me." I asked.

"Sure. That would be fun." She whispered.

As the evening was getting late, she told me she was ready to go home. I asked her if I could walk her to her car. Back in the day where I grew up, if you ask a girl that question and she says 'yes', then you have a good shot at getting her phone number.

She told me that I could indeed walk her to her car. Because of her beauty, I knew that all the guys in the club would be looking at us. My chest was stuck out proudly.

I felt ten feet tall as we walked out of the club. I asked her for her number. She put her number on a piece of paper. I was so smooth, as I placed it in my pocket. I didn't even look at it.

As she was leaving I shouted, "I'll call you tomorrow."

I pimped back to the club. My friends ran up to me and asked did I get her number. I was so cool.

"Yeah, I got it. See y'all later!" I said.

The next day I walked to the phone. I had never used a German payphone before. I had some loose change in my pocket. I looked on the phone. I saw '10 pfening' (about 7 cents), 1 mark (about 75 cents) and 5 marks (about $4.75). I thought a phone call should cost about thirty cents, so I pulled out of my pocket, four 10 pfenings coins.

I looked at the number she had written down the night before. I saw 057181172836.

"What kind of number is this? I wondered.

The number she had written looked fake. I immediately thought that she had made a fool of me.

My self-esteem was taken down a few notches. I thought to myself "Should I try to dial this number?" I took a deep breath and picked up the phone.

I finally dialed the number. There was a faint drone sound coming out of the phone. 'Toot', 'Toot'. It sounded like someone was blowing on top of a bottle.

"Wabigener", the voice on the other end of the phone said. It sounded like her but what in the hell was a 'Wabigener'. Before I could say anything the phone cut us off.

"What type of phone is this?" I screamed. "It took my 40 pfenings." Now I was upset. I took out a 1-mark coin. I stuffed it in the phone. I called the long assed number again. I heard the 'toot', 'toot' sound. Then I heard 'Wabigener' again. I yelled 'hello!' She said, "Is this you Percell?"

Relieved I said, "Hey it's me."

"Did you just call a minute ago?" She asked.

"Yes. At first I was looking at your number and I could not believe that it was yours. You see in the states we have seven digits in our number, 'click'.

The phone cut off again. Or did she hang up on me? What is up with this phone? I have used 1 mark and 40 pfening on a phone that keeps cutting me off!

It wasn't until I spent 5 marks and 40 pfening that I realized that the phone booths in Germany were timed. And that many Germans use their last name to answer their phones.

It was that kind of silliness that made us attracted to each other. She was fascinating and like no other woman that I had ever met at that point. Everything about her was literally foreign to me. She seemed to feel the same way about me. We both wanted to learn as much about each other's cultures.

I made the 45-minute drive to her house every Friday. She had a small 2-room apartment. I really do mean two rooms. One was a room where she slept, the other was a kitchen and in-between the two was a small bathroom.

Soon she started inviting me over for the entire weekend. Our routine was to go clubbing on Friday nights; shopping on Saturdays; and taking in a castle trip on Sundays. Those times were really nice. We did that for a year and a half.

When we made love, she always made me wear protection (remember this point, you will read about this topic again!). That was a little different for me. I asked her why and she told me that she wanted to be safe and not have any accidents.

3

'A meeting of the minds'

One Friday night late in 1987, before we went to our usual hangouts, I asked her what did she do for a living. She told me that she worked at the city hall in the work permits office. She informed me that if a person or company wanted to do any major construction on any building in town, they had to get a permit from her.

She complained that this type of job was not making her enough money. She was rather rebellious. A year before we met, she moved out of her parents' house and lived with her girlfriend. She told me that her mother wanted to control her life. She said that her parents had many rules and when she broke them, they ended up in an argument.

She could not take that all the rules and arguments and moved out. After living with her girlfriend for three weeks, she told me she found the apartment we were currently in.

Her money was about to run out when in 1988, her grandmother died. Apparently, she left a will and part of her money went to her. She used her grandmother's money in part to pay for her apartment.

A day that I will never forget is the day I took her to the bank. In March of 1988, Germany had some of the worst rainstorms in their country's history. She needed to pay bills and I drove her to the bank in a driving rainstorm. She showed me her savings account. It must have been somewhere near 10,000 German Marks (about 13,000 US Dollars).

I had never seen so many zeros in my life. I told myself that I would like to have that much and more one day. I was so motivated in obtaining that goal, the next month; I began to invest in mutual funds and stocks. I still invest today.

We continued dating for two years. In 1989 I received orders assigning me to Ft. Knox, KY. Up until that point, I had never met her folks. Why? She was afraid of what her parents might say about her dating an African American. She indicated that her parents would be in shock if they found out. Although they weren't prejudice, she said that they expected her to be with a German man.

Her town was a remote city off the beaten path and it was rare to see African Americans. When we walked around her city, we stuck out like a sore thumb. People stared at us all the time.

One day, we were in the city window-shopping. A friend of the family apparently saw us there. When we got home the phone rang. I could hear yelling on the other end. It did not take me long to figure out that we had been seen. Now, it was time to meet the parents.

Boy, did we meet! We were invited to their home for dinner. The house looked small on the outside. When her father opened the door, and invited us into what appeared to be a palace! I immediately noticed the rugs that hung on the walls and the spotless wooden and marble floors. Everything was neat and in its place. Pictures with family members were in small frames that were placed along a bookshelf.

We all proceeded silently towards the kitchen. She seated me next to her at the dinner table. Not one word was spoken until she introduced me in German. I wondered if they understood English. Nothing else was said during the entire meal.

After dinner, we moved to the living room. I was directed to sit in a chair that was positioned in front of the group. I felt as though I was center stage in a darkened room with one huge ass light shining down on me. Her parents peppered me with numerous questions about my intentions with their daughter.

There were a lot of translations going on between her, them and me. Her mother was upset that I had not learned enough German in the year and a half that I was there. She was annoyed that I could not communicate in their language. She also asked many questions about the US and wondered why Blacks were the cause of many crimes. She asked me if her daughter would be safe around a lot of Black Americans. You see their view of America was through the newspapers, movies and the media.

That night, I think I defended every black person in the states. After the intense grilling they began to feel more at ease with me.

Two months after arriving at Ft. Knox KY, we continued to communicate and I proposed on the phone. Because she was a German citizen, I started the paperwork for a finance visa. Once the visa was approved we had to be married within six months.

As soon as she arrived in the states, problems started.

In my mind, because she was German, everybody was against our impending marriage right from the start. Her parents, my parents, and some of my friends were against the idea of marriage mainly because of race. Some of my military friends said 'she just wants to marry you so she can get a green card.' Despite all the talk, I was truly in love with *her* and not her nationally.

In reality there were more than a few problems between us from the very start. You will read about them later in this chapter. She told me some 10 years later that we should have gone to counseling at the beginning. I knew or at least I thought our problems would work it self out in time. I thought the beginning of our marriage wasn't all that bad; we had some very good times. But you know the old saying, "you never remember the good times, only the bad."

She quit her job at city hall. We married in 1990 at my parents' house.

After the marriage, we returned to Ft. Knox, KY. We were ten hours away from Chesapeake. That was great for my parents because we could make the long trip to their house during the holidays. On the other hand, we were so far away from her folks it made them upset.

We were at Ft. Knox for three years and did not like it. The summers were ungodly hot and I worked long hours at a basic training unit. My days and nights were all in one. Somehow, we survived.

Towards the end of my tour in Kentucky, I called the Department of the Army (DA) and asked to be stationed in Germany. My objective was to relocate closer to her parents. We got an assignment to Schwabisch Hall, Germany.

We loved Schwabisch Hall but the army eventually closed the post and moved us north to Hanau, Germany. We lived eight hours away from her folks and managed to see them on birthdays and holidays.

We did not like Hanau because we lived near the Frankfurt airport and in the flight path of many aircraft. The planes flew directly over our apartment every twenty minutes or so. Right down the street from us was a tire factory. The smell of rubber was awful.

It was the spring of 1993 and we were still practicing safe sex when we had a meeting of the minds. She decided that it was time for us to have a baby. She said that the German health care was one of the best in the world. By having a child she would qualify for 'Kindergeld'. 'Kindergeld is money that the German government provides for the care of newborn babies. As she explained it to me, 'Kindergeld' was a far superior system than the American system could offer.

She also talked about the joy of becoming a mother. It took one time of unprotected sex and she conceived. **Right after conception, we went back to safe sex.** (You will read about this topic again.)

Our son was born the next year. I watched the birth and cut his umbilical cord. That was so cool; it had to be one of my proudest moments in life.

"The Bo"

When our son was born, he felt like he weighed a ton. I nicknamed him 'Pounder'. That nickname didn't stick for long. I started calling him 'Hambone'. 'Hambone' was a way of saying that he was heavy and thick boned.

The name that stuck with him throughout his childhood was 'Bo'. As he grew older, he became thinner. For whatever reason one day I just started calling him 'Bo'. I like the sound of the name. He seemed to like it as well. Hell, he would have responded to any name I picked. In returned he called me 'Papa'.

She decided to breast feed our son. I did not have a problem with that. Today's studies show that most breast-fed babies are healthier. I loved the idea that she wanted to feed him that way. (Remember this point; you will read about this topic again!).

After two years in Hanau, it was time for my next assignment. It was 1995, and in order to keep both families happy, it was my family's turn for us to go back to the states. My next tour of duty was at the Virginia Military Institute (VMI) in Lexington, VA.

When we first arrived in Lexington, we noticed how historic the buildings looked. Lexington is a small, cozy town and has many interesting attractions. Part of the civil war was fought here. Driving downtown is a virtual leap into the past.

We took a tour of the city by horse driven carriage. Overall, the town has a nineteenth century feel to it. It seems to me that Lexington is a great place to raise a family.

'This house is not a home'

We rented a house that was only a ten-minute walk from downtown. We had a beautiful view of the Blue Ridge Mountains. Inside of our small two-bedroom house were hardwood floors. When you came through the front door on the right side was the living room with a fireplace and a dining room combination. The kitchen was behind the dining room.

On the other side of the house was a 'playroom' for our son. Down the hall was a bathroom. At the end of the hall was the master bedroom and across from it was a tiny guest bedroom.

The outside of our home was picture perfect; but on the inside troubles were brewing.

My first problem I had was money. I was in a rut. I had been in the army for nine years and only been promoted twice. There were many people in the army and advancement to the top was very difficult thus making promotion almost impossible.

During this time, I was a Staff Sergeant (E-6) and bills were coming in. I was barley making enough money to keep our heads above water. My wife did not work; she wanted to stay at home and raise our son.

I wanted to get out of the army and try to make more money. However, living in a small town that prints their newspaper twice a week had few job opportunities. I would be struggling even more to make ends meet. So I had no choice but to stay in the military.

The second problem was my job. When I joined the army in 1986, my title was Unit Supply Specialist. My duties included requesting, receiving, storing, all supplies and equipment. That means in civilian terms that I managed all equipment the unit has.

So far I had been in four different units in four different places. VMI was no different. I was doing the same job. I was bored and unfortunately I brought that attitude home. Our conversations about work became routine and tedious (like my job in the army). I had nothing to talk about. Her conversations were routine as well. She'd talk about what the Bo did that day.

I needed and wanted to talk to her about my problems. Many times after a hard day of work, I tried to start a conversation. Her attention would be solely on our son. I don't think she really understood what I was going through. Her world was our son.

The third problem was our adjustment of becoming parents. We never had any time alone. I don't want to be misunderstood. I enjoyed having my son and I would play with him every moment I was awake. However my son and her were really close. In my opinion, they were too close. If she would leave the room, he tried to follow her. If she left the house without him to go shopping he'd throw a fit! Because she was around him everyday he really became attached to her.

One day, I made a suggestion we could get a sitter for an hour so we could go to dinner. She was afraid that our son would miss us.

She wanted to go on family outings. There was nothing wrong with that, but when *she* sits in the back seat with our child, now that is a problem. I felt like a Chauffeur rather than a family. One day I told her to get in the front seat with me. She did and our son started to cry. She pushed the front seat back and lowered the seat so he could touch her hair! Talk about spoiling a child!

A few months later, we traveled to Virginia Beach for a weeklong 'family' vacation. The trip was more like a '*them vacation that did not include me*', for a lack of a better term. For example, I wanted to walk on the strip and look at souvenirs; she wanted to take the Bo and walk on the beach. I wanted to eat this; she would take him to another place and eat something else.

Back in Lexington, our biggest problem was time. We never spent any time alone. Some nights we would plan on watching a movie or sit around our fireplace and chat. I cannot count how many times we were interrupted. As soon as our son cried, she'd make a beeline to him. Thus, she left me alone for the rest of the night.

Sex was a thing of the past. (We would make love once, maybe twice a month). In order to put him down for the night she had to (what else?) breastfeed him. For some reason, she would always put him down in our bedroom. One day I asked her why she was doing this. She said that she wanted to be close to him. If he woke up in the middle of the night hungry, she would be there to feed him.

I gave in and slept in the smaller bedroom. (Does this remind you my parents?). I thought that this would only last a month or two. Boy was I wrong. It lasted three years!

If we made plans to "be together", I prepared the 'playroom'. I'd light candles and get pillows to create the right atmosphere. We picked this room because it was larger than the guest bedroom. On this particular night, I got the room ready. I waited for ten minutes. I walked to the bedroom. There she was sound asleep. Thus, I was left waiting and waiting for nothing. The next day she apologized. But when it started happening to often, it pissed me off.

My verbal abuse began, and she accused me of having a temper (sounds familiar?). This was my fault and I knew better but I can say that I never laid a hand on her!

I truly don't want to paint a bad picture of her. There were times that she put the Bo down and would spend time with me. When we did make love it would be protected sex as usual. Hell, I didn't mind. I was happy to 'get it' when I could.

One night we had a long conversation. It was about time for us to be leaving the states again. She told me that she wanted to travel to an exotic place like Hawaii and asked if it was possible to be stationed there. I told her that I really did not want to be traveling again. I was tired of moving every three years and was looking at an extension of time in Virginia.

She was furious. We got into an argument. Her idea of seeing the world was through my assignments in the military. She thought that I would be excited with a possibility of going to Hawaii. To calm the situation down, I told her I would check into it. The next day I called DA and my request for Hawaii was denied.

My fathers' last months

Timing is everything, and God made it possible for me to be close to home for my fathers last few months.

Late in his life he couldn't do a lot for himself. He could not drive. He really looked forward to the days that I would drive down from VMI and take him out. He would look out the window and would marvel at all of the new construction that was going on around town. He would get a kick at the new roads or interstates that would be springing up and the new houses being built. Anything new would fascinate him.

There were times that I needed advice and I would call him. If you remember our house had a fireplace. During the winter months, I tried many times to start a fire in the fireplace. I bought those self-starting logs then put wood in the fireplace only for my fire to go out. I used kindling wood to get it going but it did not help. One day I was so mad I called my dad.

I told him my problem. He could tell I was hotter than the fire I tried to start. He said, "Have you tried small pieces wood". I came back and said, "I had chopped down the whole damn back yard for wood". He laughed so hard I ended up laughing. We laughed for about 5 minutes. Then tears came to my eyes. I realized that this was the first time we had shared a laugh in years. I will never forget that moment. He ended helping me to get that fire going. He was so proud.

Towards the end of his life his voice sounded so rasp, so weak. When I was younger, his voice was so strong, especially when he was mad.

In 1991, doctors told him he had about three years to live if he did not get a kidney transplant. He did not want one; so he went to dialysis three days a week.

The last time I spoke to him before he died, we were chatting about small stuff. As I told him to take care he told me that he loved me. That was the first time that he said that to me. I knew right then that was a special moment. A few days later, he died on January 8, 1996, his fifth year on dialysis.

After spending three years at VMI, it was time to leave. Since the Hawaii plan fell through, and in order to please her family, I begged DA to reassign me to Germany. I received orders to a place where my marriage would have no return, Stuttgart, Germany.

4

The chicken fight

In the summer of 1998, I began another tour of Germany, my third one in eight years. Stuttgart is a very large city. DaimlerChrysler's headquarters (manufacturers of Mercedes-Benz) is located in one part of the city. Porsche's headquarters is on the other side of the city.

Stuttgart is also the home of three huge army posts, which are far apart from each other. The traffic in and around the city, as you could imagine is horrible.

We quickly settled in, and I reported to my new unit. After a month there, I knew my job, inside and out.

Getting back to our relationship, there was nothing new. The Bo was quickly growing but it was the same old stuff day in and day out. We were still in an emotional and financial rut.

Maybe the wheels were off the truck (of our marriage, that is) when we got to Stuttgart, because what ever we had went south shortly after arriving in the city. Living overseas is an experience. Most everyone in the military lives in 'stairwell' apartments, and most everyone in your building wants to be in your business.

We had five families living in our stairwell. This is a fairly small number compared to most other stairwell apartments. Some apartments have eight or more families residing in a stairwell. No matter how many families reside in your stairwell, there are always those that hang out in the parking lot, snooping and looking for gossip. You really have to worry about those people. Once your business is out, it is all over the housing area.

You may know the type of person I am talking about. They pretend that they don't want to gossip, but can't wait to hear gossip just to tell you more gossip. They are the kind of person that talks behind your back and acts like your friend.

As my luck would have it, my wife became good friends with one of the most notorious gossipers in our stairwell. I cannot and will not blame this friend of hers that my marriage went south, (it was happening before we met her) but this friend added fuel to the fire.

She was nice, but always kept something stirring. She always sat outside and read those tabloid papers. She would then give them to my wife. By doing this, I think she influenced her. My wife would bring in those newspapers and read them.

One day, I over heard them talking about a celebrity. She asked my wife, "Would you leave your husband for him?"

My wife responded, "In a heart beat!"

It seemed that they were living in some fantasy Hollywood story.

One day I saw a flyer in our hallway. There was a fashion show at the Non Commissioned Officers (NCO) club on Friday night. After the fashion show, there was going to be a dance.

I wanted to try something different to get out of the house, and suggested to my wife that we should go. Reluctantly, she said yes. This was the only time; I say again, the only time my wife and I went out by ourselves since our son was born. He was four at the time.

That evening was rather lackluster. Every ten minutes, she asked me what time it was. She also indicated that we should be heading back. I finally got her mind off of our son and had a chance to dance with her. We were reminded how much fun dancing was. We thought back to the first time we met at the club in Germany. The music was pumping and the sweat was flowing. We were getting down!

Someone came inside and said that it had started to snow rather hard. This led us off the floor and into the car in record time. Because we lived twenty minutes away from the event, we had to leave and not get 'caught in a snow storm'. Half way home the snow stopped and by the time we arrived home, there wasn't any snow on the ground. Evening ruined!

I was so frustrated with my job, not getting promoted, and my own personal life that it made me crazy. So instead of getting upset because we did not spend anytime alone, or making love, or watching a movie together or do anything as a couple, I went into a shell for a few days.

This, in her eyes was terrible because I was accused of not talking enough! Damn! What can I do to change this type of life?

One night, I stayed up late. I had a pen and paper on the table. I was thinking about us. After all, I loved her and wanted to make things work. I thought about my parents. I saw the similarities and wondered to myself; 'what happened to us?' For every action there is a reaction. For every cause there is an effect. There has to be a reason why we were falling so fast. So I came up with these theories:

Cause.

- **Rushed into getting married.** When I left Germany for the first time, she came to the US on a fiancée visa. That meant we had to be married within six months. Was that enough time for her to adjust to living in the US? Did she have enough time to grasp the English language? Did we *really* understand and know each other? Did we really love each other or were we just in heat?

Effect.

If we have taken our time to get to really know each other, we *may* have not gotten married. Some people have said that 'opposites attract'. I use to believe this for a period of time, while we were married. During the first three months of our marriage, I caught myself thinking that I loved her only for *that* reason. Why was I trying to make a statement about whom I was with, *only* because she was German? Then I realized that I was crazy for thinking that way. I started to love the *person* and not the nationality. I started out wrong and tried to make up for it.

Cause.

- **Did not understand each other's cultures.** One of the biggest adjustments that I **had** to get use to was the use of the TV. Most Americans usually turn on the TV when they come home from work. Some Americans would then go to another room and change into something more comfortable. After that, you may read the newspaper or look at the news. This is a way to unwind from a hard day's work. That did not work in our house. If the TV was on, I **had** to be in front of it. Period!

Effect.

If I had taken the time to spend a few 'quiet' minutes with her, instead of watching TV, we would have become closer.

Cause.

- **Did not understand each other's cultures part 2.** I always got in trouble about time. This happened to me a lot. For example, we made plans for a family outing one-day. She asked, "What time are we going to leave?" I replied, "Oh, around 2:00 p.m." When I walked out of the house at 2:15 p.m., she was angry! She yelled, "You said 2:00 p.m.! I don't want to go now, we are starting late!" I would fire back and say, "I said 'around' 2:00 p.m." Germans are very punctual. I did not know that I had to stand outside by the car, fifteen minutes prior to us leaving. I had to get rid of 'black folks' time.

Effect.

Well, I could have shown her more respect with time. I could have also shown her that I am dependable and reliable. If I had done this, we could have gotten our outings off to a much better start, rather than an argument.

Cause.

- **Did not understand the wedding vows.** While the preacher was talking, my wife did not have a clue as to what he was saying. She could understand me, so I ended up repeating most of vows to her. She would tell me after the wedding that every time the preacher said 'Amen' she thought that he was saying 'hey man', as if somebody he knew walked by the house.

Effect.

I should have at least gotten a copy of the wedding vows a week or so before we were to marry. If she would have read them and really understood them, would we have married?

Cause.

- **No deep conversations.** We would talk but I never expressed my true feelings on any topic. When I was younger, my father never communicated with us and I was doing the same thing with her. As a child the only way I knew something was wrong was when he was yelling. Damn! I was wrong. I am sorry for that. I knew better.

Effect.

I should have learned from my father's past mistakes. If I had given at least a try on any topic, maybe I would not be writing a book in the first place!

Cause.

- **Not much in common.** When we first met, we had good times. We would be in the disco all night. We traveled from one end of Germany to the other. We visited museums, zoos and traveled to other countries. I loved the castles and she was my personal tour guide. But did she really like doing this stuff?

Effect.

I could have taken the time to find out what she wanted to do. She never objected to going to all of the above-mentioned places. I should have asked her what she would like to do on the weekends. This could have led to a better all around 'fun' time for us.

And lastly,

Cause.

- **Different views.** I had one view and she had another. She never understood my views. We always agreed to disagree.

Effect.

I should have taken more time to *listen* to her and not just hear her.

Getting back to Stuttgart, I was going up stream without a paddle. As mentioned before, my work and my life were in a rut. I just knew things had to get better with time. I had a gut feeling that if things did not change fast, my wife's interest would go somewhere or to somebody else.

During this time I was working very hard on getting my army personal records in order for the Sergeant First Class (E-7) board that was meeting in the summer of 1999. I really put an effort into getting my records up to date with a new photo, awards and other items that needed to be in that packet. I figured that if I got promoted, my wife and I could get a new lease on life. That goal would be a career milestone. I also knew that if I made the promotion, I would be getting a new and interesting job!

To make a long story short, that summer I made the promotion! Boy, was I happy! I told my family about it at the dinner table. For one small moment, we jumped around and acted like kids. We were happy! She knew how hard I had worked and it paid off. I just knew that this would be the start of a new beginning. "It's coming together, I can feel it", I said. We celebrated with ice cream. It was a rare fun family moment.

I called my army branch in Washington, DC to find out when I would be attending the mandatory school for Sergeant First Class. The school is called the Advance Non Commissioned Officer Course (ANCOC). This is a very important school. If you fail the school, cancel your career. It's over.

Coming together? Not!

As soon as the news wore off, things were back to normal. I think she did not believe that after all these years our situation could change. She was restless. She wanted new adventures. She always dreamed of traveling to some exotic beach, in some far away land. I liked the idea, but I had to complete school first.

One day, my wife met an African guy on the city bus. When I arrived from work, she was talking to her gossipy friend with excitement. When we had dinner that night I noticed she was unusually happy. She told me of her unexpected encounter with the African.

She was going to the post library to pick up some books for our child, when they met on the bus. He told her all about his county. So instead of getting books for our child, she had books about Africa and she was showing them to me while I was eating. She could tell from the look on my face that I wasn't interested.

She looked at me. "Aren't you interested in where your people come from?" she asked. "I would love to go there someday," she continued. I did not hear much after that. She was going on and on about Africa. I was trying to listen to her, but I did a quick flash back to 1988.

While I was stationed in Germany, we were planning to get married. We were lying on the floor looking at a map of the United States. I was showing her where I was from and what places I had visited. She was so excited about the possibility of going there one day. I snapped back to reality. Listening to her carry on like that, I knew some shit was up.

'A friend of the family?'

I sat back and observed things for the next few days. As my people back home would say, 'I was sitting in the cut, checkin' things out.' After a week, she was still going on and on about this guy. His sisters were supposed to be sending her stamps from Africa. "Oh, now this man has our address, so his sister can start a freaking stamp collection with my wife," I thought to myself. She told me that her and his sisters would be writing as pen pals.

The next few days I was living in a state of denial. I knew she was committed to me or at least that is what I thought. "This whole thing could be innocent" I thought to myself. "I could be jumping to conclusions; After all, my wife's only other friend is the gossipy one that lives upstairs. So she may be reaching out for a new friend."

It was late September. Stuttgart was hosting their annual Oktoberfest festival. We made plans to attend.

One day, my wife told me she had spoken with the African guy. She asked me was it all right for him to come over to our house and the four of us go downtown to the festival. Believe it or not, I said yes! I wanted to see this guy.

Mistake number one; never invite the enemy on your own turf. She told me that they were just friends and was only interested in him as far as learning about Africa.

Mistake number two; never believe your wife.

She was so excited that I said yes. She made the plans and the next day we were to meet him down the street from our house at the bus stop.

The day arrived and we walked to the bus stop. My wife paced around, as bus after bus came and went. Finally after about 20 minutes he arrived by taxi.

When he got out of the taxi, he was very slim and dark skinned. He was slightly taller than I. He had medium dreadlocks that were neat and was causally dressed.

"I apologize," as his thick African accent filled my ears. "We were caught in the middle of a traffic jam. You know how the traffic is. Were you waiting long?" Before I could answer, my wife jumped in. "No we have been waiting only a few minutes," she said. As we were introduced, I tried to break his hand when we shook.

We got on the bus and went to the festival.

The bus pulled up to the entrance and we got out. Right away they were walking together. My son and I were bringing up the rear. "I knew it!" I said loudly. "Knew what?" the Bo asked. "Nothing, "I quickly responded, "nothing at all." As the day fell into night, it was time to eat. He suggested that we get chicken from one of the vendors.

If you have been to Germany, you know that they cook an entire chicken, whole, on a rotisserie. You can have the chicken served to you in one or two ways; either whole or the vendor will take a pair of big ass scissors and cut it in half.

"Here, my friend you take the first piece of chicken," as his thick African voice boomed again. He passed the plate towards me, giving me half of chicken. "Thanks," I said. The rest of the evening was fairly uneventful. If you don't understand what I just wrote, I don't either, because the next night, that chicken, ended our marriage.

The next day the Bo, my wife and I gathered around the table for dinner. My wife was not in a talkative mood. "What's wrong?" I questioned. "Why did he give you the first piece of chicken?" she asked. "Who?" I had a puzzled look on my face. She said, "Taki (I guess that was his name). Taki gave you the first piece of chicken, why?"

I started to laugh because I thought it was a joke. I found out that she was not laughing. Right then I knew she really liked this guy. Still, I wanted to be sure, so I threw out another comment. "I don't know why he gave me the first piece of chicken. Is that their custom to serve the man first?" I shot back.

It was on then!

"You like him, don't you?" I yelled. I told our son to go outside. I did not want him to see us in what was going to be a major argument. He went out to play with his friends. She jumped up and went to the kitchen carrying a few plates with her. She never answered me. I asked again. I had no response. All of that pent up anger and frustration that I had kept inside reached a boiling point. For a quick moment I felt like my father, feeling how he might have felt many times when he used to yell at my mother. It was powerful.

I took my plate in my hand along with a bread-cutting knife and went to the kitchen. As I came around the corner I yelled, 'answer me!' I was pointing the knife at her. As she left the kitchen, I quickly 'snapped back' to reality.

My wife told me that I needed to go to counseling. She said that this was the last straw and for a long time she wanted to go but was afraid to ask. She said that she had kept ten years of pain inside her.

I went into the bedroom, feeling so guilty. I wanted to talk to her and apologize, but it was no use. I told her that I would go to counseling.

I was so amazed at this. She turned the tables on me. First, she asked me about the chicken, then I accused her of a relationship, and now I am going to counseling. How in the heck did that happen? She got off the hook because she never did tell me if she liked him or not.

A few days later we went to counseling. It was useless. Her mind was made up to divorce. She went on and on about how our bad relationship was my fault. I thought to myself, 'why are we here, if her mind is made up to divorce. The second and third time I went to counseling alone. She refused to go and indicating that it was me and not her that need help. Damn!

Once again I called DA, to find out my ANCOC schedule. I was to leave the first week of November 1999 and return in February. Again, we were excited that I received the dates for school. Maybe I was excited about school and she was excited to have the chance to be alone with her new 'friend.'

Before I left to go to the airport, I looked into my wife's face; she looked at me as if I was a stranger. I felt like I was being led off to a firing squad, and she was putting on the blindfold and lighting up the cigarette for me to smoke.

Off to school I went, knowing that something was going to be different when I returned. I had an uneasy feeling that day. While I was on the plane, I thought about her, our son and her 'new' friend. I should have been thinking about ANCOC.

5

'School daze'

While on the plane, I could not get my wife off of my mind. I wrote her a letter stating that I was sorry about our argument over the chicken episode.

On November 7, 1999, I arrived at Ft. Lee, Virginia, for school. I tried to put all of my personal problems behind me, but it was difficult. I was facing four months of physical training and studying.

The second day I was there, I found myself day dreaming and could not focus on what was being taught. I asked my instructor if I could speak a counselor. I told him that I needed someone to speak to about my personal problems.

He called a counselor. The instructor told me that he would see me after class. The counselor was only a couple of buildings from our classroom. After the last class, I met the counselor in his office.

I told him my problems. He listened and made some suggestions. I felt a little better when I left, but the next day she was on my mind again. Damn!

I started daydreaming again in class. I daydreamed about the time we were at VMI. We were in a huge argument about breastfeeding. She told me that *I* needed to go to counseling. I shot back and said that she needed to go. I told her that it was strange that she was still breasting the Bo at age three.

After the argument, I found a letter that was addressed to me. She had met a pastor and he wrote me. I don't remember the exact content of the letter, and still upset at our argument, I tore it up.

I tore up the letter because in remembering my childhood, counseling was never mentioned. Looking back on that topic, my father might have thought that counseling was a sign of a man not in control of his house.

I looked back at VMI and realized now that my wife was reaching out to me through this pastor. I missed the sign.

Soon, my classmates could tell something was wrong. I was always late in answering questions. At times I felt like I wasn't in school. My daydreams continued. My friends would ask me often, maybe too often, was I all right? They suggested that I needed to go to bed earlier.

A good night's sleep at ANCOC was impossible. We did our physical fitness at 4:30 a.m. Monday through Friday. That lasted about an hour and a half. Our classes started about 8:00 a.m. After school, which ended at 4:30 p.m. in the afternoon, my classmates and I would eat dinner.

Some days we would go to the mall and check out a movie. They were so much fun to hang out with, that you did not want to miss a day of 'messing around'. Our nights always ended up studying late or playing cards. Most of the time I was an active member of the group, but I had to talk to someone about my problems at home.

One of my friends at school was SFC Webb. One day I asked him to come by my room. I told him everything that was happening at home. It felt good to talk and get things out. He listened and told me that the world was not over. He also said that a few people in our class had problems at home. Then held told me that a few of our classmates had gone through a divorce.

I was surprised to find out that 10 out of the 28 people in my class were having similar problems. I talked to just about everyone (out of the 10) to get some type of perspective.

"Thanksgiving"

Somehow, I made it through the thanksgiving break. The break was two weeks long. I rented a car and made the thirty-five minute drive to my mom's house for a much needed break. I was both physically and mentality drained.

I arrived at my mother's house. I kissed her and told her I wanted to use the phone. It was my wife's birthday. I wanted to call her to wish her a happy birthday. I also wanted to tell her that I had spoken to a counselor and was getting some advice from my friends. When I called I could tell something was up.

"Hello, happy birthday", I said. "Thanks", she said plainly. Her voice was flat. I asked her if everything was ok. In an uneasy tone she said, "I have decided to move out. I guess you could see it coming. There is nothing left. I have had enough. I have had ten years of pain, ten long years." What I felt was in those moments was,

Panic. Fear. Lost.

This is the worst feeling I have ever experienced. As she was telling me about moving out, I could not speak. My body felt heavy. Words could not come out. I felt like ten people were holding me down, and a couple of more were holding my mouth shut.

"What do you have to say? Hello, are you there? What do you have to say? I see nothing has changed; you still have nothing to say. Why do I waste my time?" she said.

The only thing I could say was, "please give me a chance. I have learned many things about myself. Don't move out; wait until I get back from school". Her mind, like everything else, was made up. I was at the beginning of the end.

"I am a failure"

My mom knows me. She knew something was wrong the minute I got off the phone. She asked me was everything ok and of course I said that it was. This went on for two days until I could not hold it together anymore.

I woke that morning feeling like a complete failure. I got out of bed. I went to my mother's room. I sat down beside her and cried on her shoulder. This was the second time since I was seventeen I had cried on her shoulder.

The first time cried was when my first love; Kiwania broke up with me. Man, do I remember that day! I cried on my mother's shoulder for about ten minutes. I remember saying to my mother, "Please don't tell daddy." I did not want my father to think that I was a crybaby. As I have written before, he rarely showed any emotion, and he instilled that in me. He was from the 'old school'. "A man never cries; that is a sign of weakness. Always be a man," he would say.

When my father died, I did not cry at his funeral.

This time, I cried again on my mother's shoulder. After a few minutes, I went to my room, only to return to hers and cried again. "I feel like a failure," I said. My mother told me that I was not a failure. I thought about my son and realized that he would grow up without me.

I asked, "Why is this happening to me? Why is she leaving? Why is she giving up on me? Then I stated, "I am going to counseling. I have learned a lot about myself, I know I can change. I want to have one more chance. Just one more to show her I can be the man she wants me to be. I feel like a big failure. I have a family and I don't want to lose them."

After I finished, my mother broke in and said, "Your father." I knew what she was about to say, but I stopped her in mid sentence. I said, "I have repeated the same things my father has done to you didn't I?"

"From his grave he still has an effect on you." she whispered. I felt sick and lay in my mother's bed.

Later in the day, I thought I could talk my wife out of her decision. I considered on letting her sleep on it, and maybe tomorrow, I could make her understand that I am doing everything possible in saving our marriage.

The next day came. I was so afraid to call. Again, I felt sick and my stomach was in knots. It took me a long time to pick up the phone. I think I stared at the phone for over an hour. I dialed half the number and hung up. I was as afraid as to what she would say; that she did not want to be with me again.

I finally dialed the number. She answered the phone. When I heard her voice, I knew it was all or nothing. My first thought was not to make her upset. I told her everything I was doing in making our life better. Then, I eased into the topic of not moving out.

It did not work. Her mind was set. After we hung up, I went through many emotions. I was upset at myself and afraid of losing my son. Then I felt sadness. A few minutes later I felt lost. I felt it was the end of the world. On a top of all of this, I had to go back to school for another 2 months.

I did not want to see anybody. I did not want to talk to anyone. I wanted to be left alone. I was very depressed.

The two-week break was over and it was time for me to go back to school. My mother wished me the best and I made the drive back to Ft. Lee.

I arrived late Sunday evening. One of the first persons I saw was SFC Webb. He asked me how my thanksgiving break was. I told him the terrible news. He felt bad for me, after all a child was involved.

Once in my room, I tried to accept the fact that my wife was moving out. Still, I felt that when I return to Germany, I could talk to her face to face and convince her to move back in. For the next few weeks I went through a terrible cycle of hate, anger, and sadness.

"Trapped"

For the next two months I did not speak to my wife. When I called home, a German recording spoke. It sounded like she had the number disconnected.

I finished ANCOC. I graduated 12 out of 28. Not bad considering that I totally went 'though the motions' of school. I was afraid to return to Germany. I wondered how much furniture was gone.

When I got on the plane, I had random thoughts. I wondered how I would I get in contact with her. Did she move out of the city? I was adamant of not giving up on our marriage. The tragic tale is that she gave up on me. I wanted us to go to counseling. I was so willing to be the right man for her.

The plane landed in Stuttgart and I caught a bus home. Along the way, I decided that I did not want anyone to know that I was back home. I knew when my wife moved out; the nosey neighbor was watching everything. I was finally the talk of our small community.

The bus stopped near my house. I got my bags and ran off the bus and into my first floor two-bedroom apartment.

When I opened the door, the apartment was half empty. Gone were the sounds of my son playing in his room. Gone was the smell from the kitchen. Gone was the sense of family. The house was stuffy and musty. For a moment it felt like I was in my grandmother's house. I was all-alone.

I closed the door and put my bags in the dining/living room. The dining room table with four chairs was still in its place. In the living room was my TV. In the corner of the room was the grandfather clock that I had purchased before I left to go to school.

I walked towards the master bedroom. The bed was gone but she left a nightstand with a lamp in the room. I checked my closet and found my clothes.

The Bo's room was completely empty. That made me very sad.

As I made my way back to the living room, I headed towards the kitchen. She left only a few plates, utensils and one frying pan.

I stood there in disbelief. A few minutes later I remembered our upstairs room.

I ran up the stairs to the top floor. Everyone in our building had a small 'maid's room'. We had this extra room set up in case her parents would visit us. We had a double bed with a table in it. I opened the door and to my relief the bed, chair and table was there. I quickly took the bed apart and moved everything in to my apartment.

That afternoon, I found a piece of paper underneath the TV stand. There was a phone number and an address on it. It was in her handwriting. This may be her place. I waited until it got dark and ran to the closest phone booth. I talked to her and got directions to where she lived. She told me that I could take the Bo with me this weekend.

I became a prisoner in my own home. The second day I was home, my doorbell rang. I did not answer, and did not want to be seen. I stayed away from the windows. I saw my nosey neighbor with her husband sitting outside. When they went inside, I ran outside and jumped into my car to get something to eat. Then I drove around for hours. I arrived home close to 10:00 p.m.

That night, I kept all of the lights off in the house. If I needed to leave the apartment, I chose to leave under the cover of darkness. The first few days I did not eat at home, I ate fast food. For breakfast, I left early in the morning to go to the McDonald's down the street. I stayed away from the apartment until it was dark. Some days I drove by the apartment during the day to see if I could sneak in. If I saw anyone sitting out side I would drive by quickly.

When I went back to work, I left an extra half hour earlier than the rest of my neighbors. Of course I was always the last person to leave work so I would arrive home very late. Because my car was a stick shift I would turn it off when I got close to my parking lot and 'drift' into my space. I did not want to make any noise when I came home.

During the evenings I lit candles and kept them on the floor. I closed all of the drapes. Living like this wasn't new to me, this reminded me of how my grand-mother lived; in a dimly lit place.

I was so embarrassed to be home. I tried to be a mystery to my neighbors. I did not want to talk to them and feed into the gossip. I did not know how much they knew and I wanted to keep it that way. I lived like this for almost two months.

When Friday evening came around I was off in the direction of her new place. I found out that she lived only about fifteen minutes away from our apartment. And ironically enough, it was down the street from the area where the big city festival was held. If you remember from the last chapter, it was here were we went out with the African man.

I had no problems finding her place. I drove around to find a parking spot. There were so many cars around; I had to park two blocks from where she was living. She lived in the rough side of town. There were many people hanging out in the streets. I walked past a nightclub that was blasting rock music loudly. I was briefly confused and looked at the paper to make sure that this was the right place.

I was in the right place but I did not see her apartment. A few doors from the nightclub, I saw an Italian restaurant. I was about to go in and ask some one if they knew the address that was written on the paper, when I heard her voice yell-ing to me.

She lived right above the restaurant and was calling my name. She told me to walk towards the restaurant's back door. I would see a doorbell with her name beside it. She buzzed the door when I approached.

When I opened the door, I saw stairs that led up about four flights. I got to the third floor and there was my six year old son standing there with a big smile. My heart almost stopped as I noticed that he was bigger than what I remembered. He was excited to see me. He ran towards me and we hugged in the hallway. To me it happened in slow motion, just like in the Hollywood movies.

She was halfway in her apartment smiling. "He really missed you," she said. "I miss the both of you so much," I replied.

Once we got inside, I noticed that her place was really, really small. Her place was dimly lit. She showed me around. That took all of two minutes. Her bathroom had a toilet and a bathtub. In the kitchen, (get this) was her shower and sink! Beside the sink was a stove and a small refrigerator.

She showed me the Bo's room and she slept in the family room. The sofa pulled out into a bed. The other room was being rented out to another woman. I met her. She looked to be from India. They both split the utility bill. I thought to my self that if the girl wants to take a shower, she would have to do it in the kitchen.

Then I thought to myself that my wife gave up living in an apartment for free, for this! I tried to keep my face as straight as possible. But looking at things in hindsight, she must have been really unhappy living with me.

My wife told our son to take me in his room and show me some of his school assignments. Once we were safely in his room, I wanted to ask him a bunch of questions about his mom, but I decided to wait. I did not see the African guy at all, nor any of his things.

I stayed in the apartment for about twenty minutes. My wife had the Bo's overnight bag packed by the door. After he showed me his schoolwork, we left. I told her that I would have him back by Sunday night 7:00 p.m.

"Call me before you come over. I don't want you to be waiting here and I am not home," she said.

The next day, I took the Bo to our old playground park. I took him to the Post Exchange (PX) and to the zoo. We hung out all day. When it got dark, we made it to my apartment. As soon as we got in, I could not wait any longer, I was bursting at the seams to ask questions about his mom and her new friend. I wanted to find out all the dirt.

At the age of 6, my son is so 'a matter of fact' about things. I tried to get any information from him.

"So, mommy has a new boyfriend?" I asked.

"Yes," he said.

"Anything else?" I quizzed.

"Like what?" he shot back.

"Any details. Do you like him?" as I was getting frustrated.

The Bo said, "He's ok."

"Does he stay overnight all the time?" I asked.

"Sometimes, I don't know." He calmly said.

"When you go to bed, is he there?" I asked.

"Yep," he said as he was getting bored with the subject.

"So, when you wake up, he is there right?" I inquired.

"Sometimes," as he yawned.

"Well, who do you like better? Him or me?" I asked.

"You." He said.

I knew he was going to say me, but I wanted to hear all of the 'I love you and miss you' stuff.

"Does mommy say anything about me," I asked

"Nope," he said.

I wasn't getting anywhere and I decided to call off the interrogation.

As for my wife, when I was at her apartment there were no problems. We talked kindly to each other. There were a few times that I thought that we would get back together. We would chat about the old times. It felt good that we were talking and not yelling. But I did not push the situation. I wanted time to take its course.

We only talked about divorce once. We did not stay on that subject long. It put butterflies in my stomach.

During this time I never saw "Taki". I think she kept him away from me. One Friday evening when I went to pick the Bo up, my son was standing outside the door in the hallway, with his overnight bag in his hand. I figured that 'Taki' was there.

I was home for about two months when my unit informed me I had to fill an open position in Kosovo. I asked 'why me?' Only two people in my unit knew about my problems at home. That was the first sergeant and the company commander. I wanted and needed to stay home. I wanted to try to get my wife to move back in. I wanted to spend more time with my son. I did not want to go to Kosovo.

I was now an E-7. I was 'excess' in the unit. In other words, the unit does not have a 'job' for me at my rank. Now, isn't that something? I worked so hard getting this rank and now my company commander can't find a job for me!

He said, "The old job you had before you went to school, was actually an E-5 job. It would not look good on your records to be working as the supply sergeant as an E-7. There is a 'tasking' for the unit to send an E-7 to Kosovo for a six-month rotation and you are the guy. It always looks good on your records to be deployed, you know."

I could not argue with him. I have never been deployed. So I was backed up against a wall. I thought that by going to a dangerous place like Kosovo, my wife would find new respect and love for me.

I called my wife and told her the news. She actually voiced concern about my impending deployment. She told be me to be careful and to always remember that I have a family in Germany.

Hmmmm.

6

'Underway'

I began my long trip to Kosovo on the 9th of April 2000. Specialist (SPC) Cochran and Specialist Hughes drove me to the airport. We left Stuttgart around 7:00 a.m. We had directions heading northwest to Rhine Main airport. We arrived around 10:00 a.m. only to find out that we were in the wrong place. Airport personnel told us that we needed to be at the Rhine Ordinance Barracks in Kaiserslautern (also known by many US personnel as K-town or Little America).

"All deploying soldiers must go there first. Then they will fly from the military airport," the man said. We thanked him and got directions and we were back on the autobahn headed towards the barracks. We later found out that we drove right by it. Fifty minutes later we finally arrived at our destination.

I got out of the car and walked in to find out if this was the right place. The first person I saw was SFC Ferguson. She was from Stuttgart as well. We greeted each other.

"What took you so long to get here?" her husky voice boomed. "We got lost," I said. "Well, put your bags inside the large tent. Then find the admin table and fill out your paper work," she said. I walked back to the car to gather my bags. I told Cochran and Hughes goodbye and thanked them from driving me.

All deploying soldiers were living in this huge tent. The tent was deep dark green and it was in the shape of a half circle. This tent reminded me of a maintenance tent where the army would repair trucks. When I walked in, there weren't any trucks inside. I quickly noticed about two hundred cots in a row. There was no heat inside the tent and it was a little cold.

In one corner there was an old color TV that had really no color on the screen. There was a dusty old VCR that sat on top of the TV. In the other corner there was a ping-pong table and a pool table. I saw a few soldiers playing ping-pong. Ping-pong has always been a favorite sport of mine.

I walked toward the ping-pong table and saw a sign that read 'Chaplain's Corner.' There was a sofa there. I put my things on the floor right next to the sofa. I had it in my mind that I was going to sleep on that sofa later on that night.

After filling out paper work, I sat around and met other soldiers that I would be working with.

The Red Cross personnel came later in the day. They gave us a "sundry pack". The pack included lotion, soap, toothpaste, deodorant, combs, shaving crème, a washcloth, shampoo and a toothbrush.

Later in the evening I met SFC Blakeney and Captain (CPT) Burton. We seemed to hit it off right from the start. We had a lot in common and we talked about different things. I told them that I was going to be the supply sergeant. SFC Blakeney told me that he was going to be the First Sergeant; while CPT Burton told us he was going to work in the intelligence office.

As the day grew into the night I called my wife to let her know that I was all right. We spent a few moments on the phone. I spoke to the Bo and told him to be good. I wished the both of them a good night's sleep. I returned to the tent. I found out that night that the sofa I chose to sleep on had many lumps in it.

The next day, SFC Blakeney told me that our company commander, CPT Jung would like to have her supply sergeant (me) and him in Kosovo with her right away. That would mean that we would be leaving a day before everyone else. We quickly packed our bags and we got a ride to the military airport.

It was 9:00 a.m. when we arrived. The flight was due to leave around noon. The airport was full of other soldiers going to the Balkans. We got our tickets and boarded a waiting bus. The bus made the long slow ride to our airplane. Once we were there, an air force sergeant from the Georgia National Guard gave us a quick briefing. He told us to give the crew 10 minutes and we will be underway.

C-130 rolling down the strip.

We boarded an Air Force C-130. This plane was a four-engine turboprop cargo aircraft that is design for troop transport and cargo equipment. I had never been on a C-130 before. I was curious to see how it looked inside. I was the second person to board the plane.

There wasn't any insulation on the inside of the plane and thus it was rather chilly. The plane did not have regular seats, only four benches that were located in the middle of the aircraft.

As we were led to the benches, we were given earplugs. Instead of sitting from front to back, we sat in front of each other (knee to knee). It was a tight fit. We had 43 soldiers in the plane. The engines roared loudly as I put my earplugs in. We slowly rumbled down the airstrip. We lifted off and we were in the air.

As soon as we took off, two National Guard airmen passed out sack lunches. I had a ham and cheese sandwich, chips, candy and a soda. A half an hour later the airmen picked up our trash. My legs began to stiffen up. I did not want to bother the others but I needed to stand. When I stood up, I saw that there was space to stretch my legs in the back on the plane.

There was no 'walkway' or aisle. I had to walk over knees and step over people. I finally got to the back of the plane. I saw that our bags were strapped on a pallet along with newspapers and magazines.

I did not want to be cramped up for that long, so I stood most of the way. To pass by time I read and looked out the one small window that was near the back of the plane. I found myself daydreaming about the last day I spent with my wife and son. We went to the city for dinner. Afterwards we took the Bo for a long walk in the park. It was a nice family time.

We went to the city for dinner. After dinner we had ice cream. Then we took the Bo for a long walk in the park. It was a nice family time.

I knew Kosovo was going to be a learning experience. As we started our descent, I peered out the window. "This place looks normal to me," I said.

We landed at an old airport in the capital of Skopje, Macedonia. We got off the aircraft and boarded a waiting bus.

What I thought I saw in the air was 'normal' was quickly changed. I saw many military vehicles along with different soldiers from other countries standing with their weapons patrolling the runway.

I noticed that all of the military vehicles had the letters 'KFOR' on them. In our briefing on the bus back in Germany we were told that it stood for "Kosovo Forces."

There were 20 countries from all over the world tasked with protecting Kosovo. Later I will explain.

We were driven to our next destination, Camp Able Sentry (CAS). This is where we would see the first Americans in the Balkans.

7

Finally, Kosovo

After the four-hour flight, we were loaded onto the bus and no one talked. Wide-eyed I looked around. At first I did not see much. We traveled down a long street. As we approached the front gate of CAS, we were directed to the processing center.

Once at the center we received another briefing, filled out paper work and received our KFOR id cards. CPT Jung had sent Staff Sergeant (SSG) Miller and SPC McElveen to meet Blankeney and I. They officially welcomed us to the Balkans and also gave a quick tour of CAS. CAS is a very tiny camp. However, it had all the necessities to live. It included a PX, dining hall, gym and a fitness center.

SSG Miller told us that a bus would take us to Pristina, Kosovo tomorrow. She informed us that it is a two-hour ride!

"Are we going to spend the night here?" I asked. SSG Miller said that they would drive us to the shoe factory in downtown Skopje.

"The Shoe factory?" I quizzed. "Yes, the shoe factory." SSG Miller laughed. Blakeney and I looked at each other. I had to see this.

Off to the Shoe Factory

We loaded our bags in the van. Before we drove off, SSG Miller told us to lock the doors. She said that when the van stops at a stoplight, poor people would come up and beg for money or food. Some boys will try to wash your window while you wait at the light.

We drove through the city of Skopje. Some apartment complexes looked very well kept, while others didn't. We noticed a few poor people standing near the streets.

As we approached the first stoplight, I saw beggars run towards our van. Some were tapping on the windows, while other had their hands out. Towards my right side near the front of our van, I saw a woman holding a child. Her clothes were soiled and she had old shoes. I felt awful for them. It was the first time that I saw someone beg like that.

She stood in the street as if there were not any cars around. She looked towards me. "What should I do?" I asked. Before SSG Miller could answer, the light turned green and we sped off swerving away from the woman. SSG Miller told me that she used to give a few dollars to the beggars. As soon as she would do that, many more would come out and surround the van. So now she only looks straight ahead and tries not to make any eye contact with them.

We came up to another red light. This time, little boys started running towards our van. They began washing the front window of the vehicle. As they hurried to finish their work, they too stood there with their hands out.

SSG Miller explained that some families make their sons beg for money. The parents could be doing well or they may not work at all. They would send their kids into the busy street to hustle for money. Regardless how dangerous it was, they begged as long as cars were on the streets.

I wanted to know more about the shoe factory we were going to. SSG Miller explained that when NATO took this region, they found an old metal and shoe factory in Macedonia. NATO decided that the shoe factory would be an essential benefit to the operation of the war. This is where some of the soldiers are stationed. The workers at the shoe factory have left but the metal shop is still in operation and run by the Macedonians.

We finally arrived at the shoe factory. Turkish soldiers were guarding the gates. They checked our KFOR id cards and waved us through. The van stopped in front of the main building. It did not have big smokestacks or anything like that. It was a simple looking building. We walked in.

I saw many soldiers from numerous countries. There were the French, Germans, British, Danish, Spanish, Hungarians, Greeks, Norwegian, Russians, and Irish amongst other nations. I never said and heard hello in so many different languages.

Looking inside building, the factory's equipment was taken out. There were many small metal containers that lined the floor. These were used as living quarters for the soldiers who were stationed there. There were two soldiers per container. It had just enough room for two beds, two wall lockers and two chairs.

We were told that we would not be sleeping in the containers. We would be sleeping on the second floor inside of an old rusty caged area that had bunk beds that was stacked together. This was called the 'hold over' area for people only visiting there for a short time.

We climbed the stairs and I saw at least twenty other soldiers from other countries standing around the beds with some sleeping in them. I looked for an open bed and I found one near the back of the area. There weren't any wall lockers around to keep my bags in, so I had no way of keeping my items safe. SSG Miller told me that she would keep my bags in the US supply room.

Blakeney found a bunk near the front of the area sandwiched between a French solider and one from Spain. It was getting late so I unpacked only the items I needed and went to sleep.

Tomorrow we will be in Kosovo.

You are not going to believe what I am about to tell you, but if you know anyone that has spent any amount of time in the shoe factory, they will tell you that this next part is *very* true.

As morning approached, I was awaked by someone's alarm going off. I checked my watch at it was 5:30 a.m. We were not due to leave until 9:00 a.m. so I rolled over to go back to sleep. Another hour past and someone's alarm went off again. Frustrated, I got up, wiped my eyes and walked to the bathroom. As I open the door, still groggy from last night' sleep, I saw two women at the sink brushing their teeth. Surprised and embarrassed, I thought that I had walked into the women's bathroom.

I quickly ran out of there, thinking that I would be in trouble for walking into the wrong bathroom. I looked around to find the men's bathroom. I walked back to the other end of the floor thinking that I had past it on my way to the first bathroom.

I saw people in their bathrobes with towels across their back walking to and from the same direction of the bathroom I just ran out of. I asked a man who had just stepped out of his container where the bathroom was. He pointed in the direction I just came from!

I found out that the bathroom, to include the toilet and the shower, was unisex!

After that shocking event in the bathroom, the rest of the time at the shoe factory was, for the most part, normal. I found the place where they served breakfast, which was the standard serving of eggs and bacon.

It was time for us to leave. We told SSG Miller and SPC McElveen good-bye and boarded the bus. After an hour, we arrived at the boarder between Macedonia and Kosovo. "Another hour to go", I said to myself.

As we crossed in Kosovo, there were many potholes in the road. There were a few cars that were burned out and in the middle of the streets. There was a lot of trash in the fields. I saw many people that walked along the side of the road. Some traveled by tractor and others by horse and carriage.

I saw a guy driving a car that had no front window and the top of the trunk was ripped off. I spotted another car's hood that was completely gone. Many cars did not have license plates. They were weaving all over the road as to avoid the potholes.

Twenty minutes later, I saw a sign that read "Pristina. One kilometer". As the bus went over a small hill, there it was, the city of Pristina.

8

In the Box

It was April 11, 2000 when I arrived in the capital of Kosovo. Although the sun was shining, Pristina had a gloomy look to it. It was so gray! It was not much to celebrate considering that this city had just been through a war.

Destruction and trash were everywhere. As we crossed a narrow bridge, I saw what looked like to be a military barracks. There were many trucks that were blown apart. The barracks were 'pan caked' or flatten from top to bottom. Across the street from the barracks was an oil refinery. NATO bombs took out that refinery and the barracks.

We dropped these bombs to get rid of the Serbs, and it worked. About 150 feet from the oil refinery were houses untouched by the bombings. Talk about pinpoint bombings; this was amazing.

The bus made a slow climb up an unpaved road. It looked like many trucks and cars went up the hill and all other vehicles traced their path as not to cut across what might have been a field of unexploded bombs.

We arrived at the front gate. The Hungarians soldiers checked our KFOR id cards. We crossed the front gate and I heard a loud clang. The steel gate closed and I realized that I was now inside of 'the box'.

The military term, 'the box,' refers to a hostile area.

For some reason when I heard the gate shut, I got nervous. I realized I was in a very dangerous place.

Blakeney and I got off the bus. I noticed that there were many different uniformed soldiers. I saw the French, Germans and, Turkish soldiers. Also we noticed the Russian, English, Spanish, Norwegian, Swedish, Belgium, Irish, Finnish, Ukrainian, Italians, and the Canadians. There were soldiers from all over the world. It was like the Olympics of the military.

Out of all of those soldiers that we saw, I did not see one American. For a minute I thought that we were in the wrong place. I told Blakeney to watch our bags. "I will try to find some one to point us in the right direction", I said.

I walked around the camp. I saw a sign that read, 'film city information'. I knew that we were in the right place. While in Macedonia, I remembered some one saying to me that Pristina's camp is called 'Film City'.

I looked in the first office. I saw a French soldier. "Do you speak English?" I said. He said something that sounded like "Wee, wee," ("Yes" in French). I asked him where the US soldiers were. He pointed out the door and said, "To your left." By the time I approached SFC Blakeney near the van, he was talking to the American First Sergeant.

He shook my hand as we were introduced. "First Sergeant, this is SFC Artis the new supply sergeant," Blakeney said. The First Sergeant took us to our company, the United States National Support Element (US NSE). This will be our temporary home, in the box.

Paris, 108

The outgoing First Sergeant explained what the NSE does. He told us that we would support 150 Soldiers, Sailors, Airmen, and Marines here in Pristina. There is a Company Commander (Captain Jung), First Sergeant (Blakeney), Supply Sergeant (me), administration clerks, and a mail clerk.

My main function was to issue and turn in military equipment. Additional duties included traveling to Camp Bondsteel (45 minutes away), to pick up sundry items for the US service members stationed at Film City (the 'Stars and Stripes' newspaper, cases of microwave popcorn, sodas, water and ice cream).

Located right behind the NSE was a dayroom that had a wide screen TV, pool tables, foosball table and a VCR. When the American soldiers got off work, they could come by the NSE to check their mail. The dayroom was open for them to pickup a newspaper, play a game of pool, drink a soda, pop some popcorn or watch TV.

Blankeney and I were led on a quick tour of the camp by the First Sergeant. We walked in front of an old yellow building. Before the war, the building was used to make old propaganda movies. This is how 'Film City,' got its name.

I asked the First Sergeant where are the morale phones located. He pointed to the main building and said, "You should have no problems finding it." You will see a long line. They just put ten phones in there last week and I heard some people were waiting in line for almost two hours."

We then went to the housing office. We asked for our room assignments. A French supply sergeant told us there were not any rooms available. He said that we would be living temporarily in a tent that was located on the other end of Film City. I was so tired at this point that it did not matter where we slept.

"Come back in two weeks and I should have a room for you," as his heavy French accent filled the room. We went to the tent and found a couple of empty beds. There were no lockers to store our things so we kept personal items locked in duffle bags under our cot.

The next day I walked into the main building to use the phone. The First Sergeant was right. The line ended at the front door. I decided to wait and try to use the phone at night. I went to bed early and I woke up around 11:00 p.m. As I got closer to the building, it seemed to me, as the line did not move from earlier that day.

After two weeks, Blakeney and I went back to see the French supply sergeant. He gave us a room. He said, "Pairs 108", as he pointed to the map that had all of the names of the 'barracks'. There was 'Rome', 'Berlin', 'Washington', and 'London' along with 'Paris'.

We got the key and walked to our barracks. Once we opened the door we noticed that the room contained three beds. The room was very cramped. Our roommate came in and to my surprise he was wearing a German uniform.

In his broken English he told us his name. We shook hands as he made his way past us. We spoke mostly German since he only knew a few words in English. Coincidentally, all three of our wives were German.

I left the conversation and walked over to the main building. For some reason there were only three people ahead of me. I asked the soldier who was in front of me about the long lines. He told me that most of the nations now have their own morale phones.

After a ten-minute wait, I called my wife. She answered the phone. The only word that I got out of my mouth was 'hello'.

Her voice was hysterical. "I was worried about you. Are you all right? I did not hear from you, I thought the worst!" she said.

I calmed down her fears and had a very nice talk that evening. After the call I thought that our future started to look better.

9

"You have 10 minutes"

History is my favorite topic. I have always been fascinated about how countries came into being. Since I was here in Kosovo, I set out to find what led the NATO Forces here.

In 1968, the Albanian people voted to change the name of Kosovo-Methoija to Kosovo. They also voted or demanded that Kosovo be free from the Yugoslavia/Serbia republic. The Albanians wanted to live their lives free and independent. The Serbians did not want rejected the idea.

From 1968 to 1999 there was much unrest in this country. The Serbian Republican Party dissolved the Kosovo assembly in 1990. The Serbs imposed martial law. Tens of thousands of Albanians in Kosovo lost their jobs. On a top of that, the Serbs wanted the Albanians to speak their language; Serbian. The Serbs tried to force their religion (Serbian Orthodox) on them. The Albanians (who are Muslim) refused.

In 1997, Serbian police crushed an Albanian student demonstration. Fighting in Kosovo between Serbian troops and the Albanian people began in 1998. Since the Albanian people refused to speak Serbian or practice their religion, ethnic cleansing began.

The international community could not stand by and let ethnic cleansing happen. The Serbian president, Slobodan Milosevic, was compared to Hitler. We bombed Kosovo for 78 days to drive back the Serbian army. They retreated back to Serbia.

The Lucky ones

The unemployment rate in Pristina is very high. Many households are supported by one income simply because jobs are scarce. Some of the lucky ones worked at Film City as cleaners and laborers. These are the types of jobs that most people in the States wouldn't take. The fortunate ones who spoke more than one language served as interpreters. Many stocked the PX shelves and were cashiers. Few of them work as assistant managers. Those who worked in the PX spoke perfect English.

Many of these workers had advanced degrees in engineering, finance, etc. They all needed money to survive and support their families. Regardless what their education credentials were, they were glad to do any kind of work to make it happen.

In my opinion, it is an understatement to say that the Albanians are happy to see the United States and the other countries assist them. Albanians were getting killed, taken prisoner, and forced out of their jobs and homes.

Some days we were allowed to shop at the local stores, which were about 500 yards from the Front Gate. On my way out, I always stopped at the PX to purchase a bag full of candy.

Albanian children were always hanging around the Front Gate waving to the soldiers. Usually there was a translator nearby who would ask the children for me, "how many of you went to school today?' Every time, they all would raise their hands.

I would reward them a piece of candy. Some days I gave them old army patches or rank. On hot days I treated them ice cream. It made my day to see their faces light up and to hear them say, "They say 'thank you very much.' The experience was unbelievable and made me realize just how fortunate we Americans are. We have been blessed! Let me give you an example:

I befriended with two young Albanian men that worked at our PX. Valon (17) and Fisnik (18) have seen first hand the immense hatred the Serbs have for the Albanians. They told me their amazing story:

The two teenagers lived in the same apartment building. They were best friends living under the rule and thumb of the Serbian military. When the Serbs started their ethnic cleansing, one of the first places they visited was the apartment building that Valon and Fisnik lived with their parents and siblings.

The two young boys were walking home from school one day and noticed quite a few Serbian military soldiers around their apartment building. They told each other goodbye and they would see each other later on that night. A few minutes later Valon heard a knock on the door. It was the Serbian military. There were three men armed with rifles. One man told Valon, "You have 10 minutes to get out of your apartment. If you are here when we get back, you will die right here."

Valon told his parents what the man said and they hurried to get their belongings together. The men then went to Fisnik apartment and told his family the same thing. When Valon's family ran down the stairs, he noticed that many of their neighbors were standing in front of the apartment complex with suitcases in hand.

The Serbs came back with a bus and told the families to get on. They were afraid and no one talked. The bus drove them to the Kosovo-Macedonian border. They were dropped off. There they stood in what was called the safe zone for two days. The two best friends were separated. Valon and his family spent 12 days at the Stennkovec refugee camp. From there his family stayed with a Macedonian family that they didn't know. For the next 3 months that was their home.

The two friends lived only 30 miles apart. They were unaware as to what happened to each other. Fisnik spent months in the small city of Gostivar with a family that they did not know. The times were very tough," Fisnik said. Two strange families were forced to live together in a house that was too small.

In response to the Serbian's attempt at ethnic cleansing, the US provided military assistance. We bombed the Serbians for 78 days straight and drove them back into Serbia. As the Serbs were leaving, they tried to destroy every thing in their wake. Cars, houses and cattle were burned. They planted land many mines.

Twenty-two days after the bombings ended, Fisnik and his family were placed on a bus. Get this; they were charged 20 marks (about 10 US dollars) per head to ride back to Pristina. One day later, Valon and his family arrived back to their apartment. The Serbs took Valon's TV, VCR and family heirlooms. Windows were broken.

At Fisnik's house, their cameras were taken; pictures of family and friends were smashed. Their front door was kicked in and there were holes in all the walls. Both houses needed so much work that it took about four weeks to get things back to normal.

The shock of the incident was still fresh on their faces. Valon sadly told me that his father was once the picture of good health. Since their return home, he is a broken man and has yet to recover from the ordeal. Valon was the only one working in the family because his mother had care for the father.

I don't want to give the impression that all Serbian people are bad. Some of the Serbian people were living in Kosovo at the time when the cleansing started. They were friends of the Albanian people, but they were caught between a rock and a hard place.

There is deep hatred between the Serbs (who are living in a 'controlled' area) and the Albanians. Today, Serbs churches are guarded 24 hours a day. The Swedish army is tasked to guard all Serbian churches. If the Swiss army leaves that church unprotected, the Albanians would destroy it.

I saw the remains of ethic cleansing. I was surrounded by two cultures that hated each other. I felt the prejudice and the hatred of the people. I have seen the destruction of lives, buildings and the burned out cars. I have seen the people, shook their hands and looked in their faces. We may not speak the same language but we know why I was there.

It made me feel proud that I was making a difference in someone's life. I keep jumping on how much we are blessed, but now for the first time in my life, I really understand it. There are many people suffering around the world.

In my mind, America is lucky to have problems that can not be compared to what these people have lived through. My experience made me better realized the importance of family and friends. My eyes were opened wider.

Some may say that a leopard can't change it spots. It's true. I am no leopard, but my deployment changed my views about the world and myself. The experience helped to strengthen my abilities to display compassion and consideration for others. I hoped that my wife would notice my change too.

10

"Who is in charge?"

Who is in charge of Kosovo? Who should anyone call when there is trouble? What happened to the police forces that were here? Slobodan Milosevic fired the top person in Kosovo's government down to the lowest official. He installed his own government officials after the Serbs took control.

After our bombs fell, there was no electricity or any traffic lights. The stores were looted, and crime was rampant. There were fires in the city and untrained people that tried to put them out. So, who is in charge? Who is the police and who is the fire chief?

The UN has paid a lot of money to help the people of Kosovo with homes, electricity and a police force. Some day the UN will assist the people to elect their own officials to run the government.

First, the UN had to restore order. There were four pillars that structured the mission in Kosovo (Overseas Security Cooperation in Europe (OSCE), United Nations Humanity Committee of Refugees (UNHCR), Civilian Military in Cooperation (CIMIC) and the United Nations Mission in Kosovo (UNMIK)).

One of the first things the UN did was to establish a police force on the ground. The police force (UNMIK) was made up of law enforcement personnel from 43 countries. I spoke to an UNMIK police officer from San Jacinto, California. He indicated that there were 4,759 UNMIK around the world of which 3,600 were in Kosovo.

There are certain requirements you have to meet in becoming an US UNMIK police officer. In order to qualify as a UNMIK police officer, one must have at least 8-years of experience in law enforcement and a clean record. You must also volunteer for an overseas assignment lasting 365 days or more.

The US UNMIK were paid handsomely. Their benefits included tax-free exemption, 75 dollars a day for housing and food and a 10% finishing bonus for staying the entire year.

11

"Gratitude"

In this next chapter, I want to dedicate it to the many US civilians that are here. They make our lives so much easier. They have left their families, friends and love ones behind to help us, the American solider, sailor, airman and marine live, eat and sleep comfortably. These are the unsung heroes; they are put in harms way every day. I am so grateful that these people are here with us.

I remember it like it was yesterday. When I was a pre teen, I used to listen to the number one AM radio station in Chesapeake, Virginia all the time. The radio station was named WRAP AM 850. One of the most popular disc jockeys of the early seventies was a loud, high-pitched voiced man named 'Daddy' Jack Holmes. He was the morning man at WRAP. His time slot would be from 6 a.m. until 9 a.m. I was so moved by the music and the disc jockey that I fell in love with the music (this might explain why I got into radio a few years later).

During this time my favorite group was Earth, Wind and Fire (and still is!). I started collecting their albums. When WRAP announced that Earth, Wind and Fire had a new album that was coming out, I bought it. One day I was in the record store, looking for older Earth, Wind and Fire albums that I did not own. I found a white double album entitled *Gratitude*. It was one of their first live recordings and it became one of my favorites albums.

I wondered why E, W& F named their album *Gratitude*. They had money, fame, cars and women plus they were a great group. As I grew older I found out what 'gratitude' really means. Thirty years later, I have a better respect for the word.

As I written earlier, this chapter is dedicated to the civilians that are in Kosovo. These people make our jobs much easier. They put their lives on the front lines everyday. Most of them don't even have a weapon that will protect them when they travel over the roads.

A big thanks

The Red Cross: I have come to learn that they are a great organization when one is deployed. When I travel to Camp Bondsteel, they give us our newspaper, *The Stars and Stripes*. They also give us cases of popcorn and pass out our magazine the Army, Marine and Air force Times.

They give us cold water to drink with a friendly smile. One of the employees there gave me the idea to get in contact with my Red Cross in my hometown of Chesapeake. I did. They sent me a 'goodie box' with my hometown newspapers, cookies, videotape and a surprise gift from my mom.

A side note: I can't tell you enough how important it is to get mail while you are deployed; it raises your spirit one hundred percent.

Brown and Root: These people are the best! These are contracted men and women from the states, which build the rooms and offices we work in. They cook our food, pave the roads, give us light, give us the internet café, the gym equipment, TV's, pool and ping pong tables, and well, you get the point.

You cannot image what a job these men and women do for the military. With their headquarters based out of Texas, these people are the supervisors of the construction, electrical, food preparation, road building and everything else that affect the military.

When I first arrived in Film City, there was not much to the place. We were knee deep in mud. Most of us lived, worked and ate out of tents. I met the guys from Brown and Root. They told me that in a few months, this place would be nice.

That was back in April; and by mid June we had a gym, dayroom (with morale phones) and new offices. They brought in the generator and air condition crew and made us feel cool.

When they arrived, they changed a lot of things for us. Man, do I ever appreciate walking on sidewalks, eating great food, taking hot showers and sitting in an air-conditioned room. It is the small things we take for granted living in the states. I tip my hat to these people that also left their families behind to make our lives easier. There was so much I used to take for granted; now I definitively have a different out look on life!

The people at Brown and Root made our lives easier. Not only do they serve us in Kosovo, but Macedonia, Bosnia and other parts of the world.

MWR: (Morale, Welfare and Recreation) These people bring us celebrities, concerts and plays from all over the states. They also show movies at the theater for free. The concerts are normally are once a month. The movies are three times a week. They also pay the bill for us to get the *Stars and Stripes* **free**.

AAFES: (The Army and Air Force Exchange System) Better know as the 'PX' The PX is the place where we buy personal items, movies, electronic items and magazines.

UNMIK, OSCE, CIV POL, UN: They make up all the other people from the US and other countries that keep everyone in Kosovo safe. And get this: other than the UNMIK, every organization that I have mention ***does not*** carry weapons!!!!

The other countries soldiers on Film City always had something going on at their unit (NSE), and often times we were invited. I am grateful for meeting so many different people from all over the world. It's hard to believe that I was in Kosovo, in the middle of a war zone. We worked hard, and played hard.

If you think about it, we all have a lot to be grateful for. If you have not been to a deployed area here at least two things you will notice right away.

The first item you will notice is the noise. Generators run everything and they are loud. You have to remember that all electrical cables are not on a pole or buried in the ground. They are placed neatly on top of the ground and covered with boards or tarps.

These generators run lights and air condition in the room, the PX, the gyms, offices, tents and the dining facility. These generators are everywhere and they run 24 hours a day. My first few nights at Film City, was very uncomfortable, I did not get much sleep because of the generators. Believe it or not you will get use to it; you have to or you will never get any sleep.

Another noise factor to consider are the many helicopters that land day and night at Film City. There were many missions along with dignitaries that traveled through out Kosovo.

The second thing you will notice is that you don't have any privacy. As I have written before, my first few weeks at Film City, was rather rough. When I wanted to talk to my wife on the phone there were long lines. Many of the nations used the morale phones that were located in one small room.

There were about 10 phones on a long table. There was a sign up sheet at the entrance of this particular room that clearly read, 'Phone use is ten minutes only'. Very rarely did anyone abide by the rules. Some people talked so loudly that you were listening to their conversation rather than your own. This made it hard to talk to my wife about anything *and* do it in less than ten minutes.

Three months later, the Americans had our own morale phone room. This made it a little easier, but still talking about delicate issues to my spouse around other waiting soldiers was uneasy. Two weeks after that, I told the first sergeant that I needed more privacy. I asked him if I could use his phone so I could talk longer with my wife. He agreed.

Writing letters was also very difficult. With the noise of the generators and the cramped room space, I wanted to be alone with my thoughts when I put pen to paper. Many times I would stay in my office well after hours so I would have time to reflect, write notes for this very book, or write a letter.

Could you imagine living like this for a long period of time? I know you would adapt and I hope you can see by these two small examples that we have so much to be grateful for.

12

What the hell is going on?

I had been deployed for four months. My wife and I talked on the phone at least twice a week. Our conversations had been very nice. I informed her as to what I was doing in Kosovo. I told her about the people that I had met and passed along some of my experiences as well.

She was very enthused and I mentioned that I could write down some of the things that I had been doing. I suggested that she could read some of my stories to the Bo for his 'bedtime' stories. The last few chapters of my book were for him.

I stayed off the subject about 'Taki'. I never asked about him. She never mentioned him as well. I passed it off as just a fling.

I did however bring up the subject about moving back in with me. One day she told me that she would wait until I got back home. She said that she could not move all of the furniture 'by herself'.

The Bo sounded great as well that day. He talked to me for a long time. He told me that he missed me and wished that I were there. After that phone call, I felt good about our future. I had dreams of us becoming a family again.

I did not want to mess up my 'high' about my family. I decided to wait a week and call them. I figured the less I called the more we would have to say.

I waited about a week. Excited, I dialed the number and she answered. As soon as I said hello, she yelled for the Bo and told him that I was on the phone. This puzzled me because we normally chatted a few minutes before she passed the phone to him. It made me suspicious.

"Hey Bo. How is my big man doing today?" I asked.

"Fine." He said plainly.

"Is mommy's boyfriend there?" I asked.

"Nope." He said.

I was relieved. I could just see my heart jumping out of my chest if he told me that 'Taki' was there.

"He was here last night." The Bo volunteered.

I was stunned. I picked my heart off the floor. I asked to speak to his mother. I told myself that we have got to get this thing settled right now. As the Bo called his Mom to the phone, I asked myself 'what can I do about this problem, if I am in Kosovo.

She came to the phone. I had to choose my words carefully. I tried to eased into the topic.

"The Bo told me you had a visitor last night." I said.

"Yes. He did not stay long. He got some of his clothes. I don't know about him."

Like a dummy I asked, "Is there a problem?"

"Yes. But you don't have to worry. You have a job to do there. Keep writing those stories for us."

I said, "I hope you can see that though these stories I have become a new person with expressing my thoughts on paper. I know in the past I had been accused of not having much to say. I thought it would be different to write things down. Although I have never talked about my true feelings much, I wanted to show you that I was coming around to becoming someone different. I wanted to paint a picture of what was happening in Kosovo and how those things are affecting me."

She said, "Yeah, sure. Someone is at the door, I have to go."

That was the end of our conversation. I hung up the phone hoping for a miracle that things were finally working in my favor.

Or is it and who was at the door?

Hmmmm.

13

'The Papa Chapters'

These are quick mini stories for my son (who calls me papa). Some of these are 'firsts' for me and others are not.

Papa and the Helicopter. Often we had to go back to our rear detachment in Skopje, Macedonia. We had about 20 to 30 soldiers stationed there. By shuttle bus, it took about two hours to get there (on a good day). As written before the roads are filled with potholes and are rather dangerous.

When I rode the bus, my biggest fear was when we got to the mountainous area. There were no guardrails. This made the trip very unnerving. We also had to travel through a long, dark narrow tunnel. The bus had very dim headlights. During the time we were in the tunnel, I always prayed that there was no on coming traffic.

No matter how bad the roads were once you get to the mountains the view was wonderful. It's hard to believe that in a place like this, there was a war only 5 months ago. Once you crossed into Macedonia, the road got better.

A faster way to get to Macedonia was by helicopter flown by the Ukrainians. The UK-47 HIP helicopter was nicknamed by Americans as 'old shaky'. The helicopter 'shuttle' ran daily between Pristina and Skopje. The trip took 30 minutes.

One day I had to attend a meeting in Skopje and missed the shuttle bus. I had never flown in a helicopter and I thought to myself, there was no way I was going to get into that metal spin box named 'old shaky'. Upset at myself, I signed up for the helicopter shuttle anyway. I was nervous.

When I got in, I noticed that it seated about 20 people. It had plenty of leg-room. Once everyone was on board, and the engine started, I quickly found out why we called it 'old shaky'.

That helicopter shook and shook, as we were about to lift off. I was so scared, I had my eyes tightly closed and it felt like my stomach was going through my mouth. I must have had a terrible look on my face. A gentleman that was sitting next to me tapped me on the shoulder. I open my eyes and I saw him smile at me as he was pointing towards the window.

We were still on the ground. I felt embarrassed. Once we lifted off, the view was wonderful. I took plenty of photos and had a great time.

Papa and the Dentist. I started to experience pain in my mouth. I feared that my wisdom teeth have finally caught up with me. Before deploying my dentist suggested that I have my teeth removed but since they didn't hurt at the time, I declined.

That day, I was in so much pain that I wanted every tooth pulled. I did not feel up to the 45-minute drive to Camp Bondsteel where the American dentist was. I knew there was a British dentist 10-minutes away located in the British sector of Kosovo.

The dentist office was located in the military hospital, which was a big green tent that was shaped like a half-oval. It was very, very clean inside. A voice boomed from behind a curtain. "Are you here to see the dentist? Take the seat over there and fill out the paperwork." I was surprised when a tiny young nurse came from around the curtain. I filled out the forms. "Are you quite finished with the paperwork?" she said. "Here you go" I replied, it was tough to talk.

"You can go down to see the dentist now. Just around the corner a bit, then wait by the empty chair there," the British nurse said. I laughed to myself as I tried to imitate the voice.

As I sat there, my pain went away. It was completely gone. I even forgot what side of my mouth had the problem. It's funny that, at least for me, when I go to the dentist, right before I sit in the dentist chair, the pain goes away.

"You are next", the nurse said. I told her that my pain went away. "That is what they all say. Let's have a look, shall we?" she said. I sat in the seat, as she leaned the chair back. Captain Carson is your dentist," the attractive nurse said.

As the assistant turned on the high beam light a voice came from behind me. I heard, "OK, relax and open your mouth". The voice was another woman! I did not remember seeing two assistants standing around. I paused before I opened my mouth. I was trying to see around the bright light. "Please open a bit," she said.

I broke my silence, "Are you the dentist?"

"Yes I am, now open please", the voice said. She could tell I was confused. So she introduced herself to me. "I'm sorry. My name is Captain Carson." She stood in front of the light. I could barley see her. I finally opened my mouth. She looked at my teeth.

"Which tooth is it?" she asked. Since I was feeling no pain, I said, "I think this is the side."

"This side?" She reminded me of my sore tooth. "Yes!" as I almost screamed the answer.

She laughed a bit. She took another look. "Yes, I see it now. It looks as if you have an infection. Infection is quite common in a deployed area. You have a large cavity and not much tooth left. I think if I pull it, your mouth should not give any problems," the Captain said.

She told the nurse to get some instruments from the back. Then Captain Carson sat me up in the chair. The first thing I noticed (other than she was another beautiful woman) was she was no taller than 5 feet.

As we waited, she asked me where I was from in the United States. "Virginia." I said.

"I have never been there before. I studied at UCLA for four years. I loved it out there in California." she said.

I asked her how tall she was. She laughed and replied, "Everyone wants to know how tall I am. Most people think that I am not a dentist. I am 4 foot 11 inches. I think that I could be a children's' dentist."

I told her that I was writing a story about my experiences in Kosovo and asked her if I could include her in my book. She jotted on a sheet of paper, Captain Madalina Carson; SDO Dental Section. The rest of the appointment was a lot of pulling and yanking of my tooth.

Papa and the UNMIK. I became good friends with the men from the United States' UNMIK police force. One night they invited me out to dinner.

We were set to leave Film City at 7:00 p.m. This was to be my very first opportunity to really see how Pristina looked. When I traveled to Camp Bondsteel every day, the main road does not go directly into the city.

As we approached the city, the first thing I noticed was how bad the roads were. There were big potholes in the streets. Cars were swerving around the potholes. It was a miracle that we did not have a head on collision.

There was trash everywhere. We saw kids playing in the middle of it as if it was a playground back in the states. The buildings were covered with black dust and the air smelled like a combination of everything bad. People were walking around appearing unfazed by all of the things I noticed. It was like any other day to them.

We arrived at our destination at 7:20 p.m. We parked the car and walked up the street. About 100 feet was a pizzeria. I wondered how the food was going to taste. I remembered all the things I saw in the city and already I had a certain prejudice about the food I was about to eat.

We walked in and to my surprise the pizzeria looked brand new. It was nicely decorated with paintings on the wall. Music played on the speakers and they had a small waterfall in the back of the room. My prejudice went out of the window. I thought that in a city like this, there was no way that a pizzeria could be this clean.

The rest of the night was memorable. We laughed and talked until 9:00 p.m. The food was excellent. The UNMIK paid for the food. I always say that 'the best food is free food!'

After dinner, I toured the police station. I saw many photos of the city and some photos of horrific traffic accidents.

I traveled with the UNMIK on another memorable trip. They invited me to a barbecue and gave me their official police patch. On it is written: 'Sunny Hill. Police in Kosovo. Department Two'. I was honored to receive a gift like that.

14

'Divorce…damn'

I always looked forward to the evenings. It was during this time that I found peace and comfort and had a chance to reflex on all the things that were around me. After dinner, I would go back to my place of work and turn on the radio and relax. Then I would turn on my laptop and write.

I had never written so much in my life. I found it easy to express my feelings. I was at one with my laptop. It felt good to write about my about my childhood and personal problems. This was a form of therapy for me.

I started to express feelings that I never expressed before. I rediscovered myself, and in the process a huge burden was lifted from my shoulders. I sent copies of my writings to my mother. She expressed more than once, how she could see that my deployment was good for me. I hoped my wife could see this as well.

My spirit was up a little until I called my wife in early August. Her voice sounded strange. I asked if there was something wrong. She said she had to talk to me. To spare all of the details, she told me that she was pregnant with her boyfriend's child. I cannot tell you what I said, but this is how I felt;

Shock. Despair. Disbelief. More shock

I really could not believe it! I could not speak. I could not believe my ears. I could not believe what was happening to me. I could not believe how my life was turned upside down, and inside out. Reality really began to set in and I knew that there was no chance that we would ever get back together.

Why did she put me through ten years of ***protected*** sex? She meets a guy and in less than a year she is having his baby!

Then I heard the most unbelievable thing in my life.

She told me that she was sorry and it was a mistake. Then my wife suggested that *we* get back together. She said that she read some books that said most husbands in this situation had treated the unborn child like their own!

If I was not speechless, I would have asked if she had lost her mind!

I did not recover from the devastating news; I told her that I was going to call back in a few days. I really did not have anything to say to her. I felt so disgusted. I wanted to throw up.

The best description of how I felt at the time was to say that I was not 'here'. My mind was somewhere then everywhere but it wasn't in Kosovo. I did not know where to turn.

When I was in the tenth grade, I had a girlfriend. By the time we were seniors in high school, she was pregnant with my child. I was seventeen at the time. I thought that I was a man. My parents were furious at me. My father told me 'because you think you are a man, you will take care of your child. Not me'.

My girlfriend and I broke up a year later.

My daughter was born in 1979. I saw her off and on for the first six of her life. That stopped when I joined the army in 1986. After my father died in 1996, we began a close father and daughter relationship.

I called my daughter and told her the terrible news about my wife's new pregnancy. I wanted to ask her opinion on this situation.

"What do you think? Should I stay for my son's sake? Or should I go through with something I am strongly against, a divorce. I know I should get one. My trust with her is out the window and without trust you don't have love." I said. I told her that I did not want the Bo to grow up without me, like I did when she was born.

She responded, "Your situation is different than ours. You were not around as much when I was born," my daughter said. "You have been around your son for six years and he will not forget you. You can visit him and maybe he will stay with you when he gets older". My daughter concluded, "It's best that you get a divorce."

I knew that, but I did not want to accept the fact that all of this was happening to my marriage. I guess I should have seen the writing on the wall. By now I sank into my deepest depression I had ever experience. I did not want to look into anyone's face. I felt that I was the worst person in the whole world. I did not have any confidence with anything that I was doing in Kosovo.

I asked God many times 'why me'? I felt like I was spinning out of control. While in Kosovo, I never let on to anyone what was happening to me. I kept it all inside for weeks. I wanted to talk to somebody, but I was so embarrassed. I didn't want to tell any of the 'guys'; I was afraid that they would laugh at me. I was also afraid that I might break down and cry in front of them.

I wanted to get a woman's prospective on my situation. I needed someone that I could trust.

At Film City, there weren't many women to choose from. I narrowed my choice to two; both of them were from my home state. One was in the military and the other was a civilian.

The female military member did not have much free time. One day, I asked her to stop by and talk to me after work. She did not show up. After asking three times, I gave up. I guess she thought that I was trying to 'pick her up'. Now I knew I was really in deep trouble. I began to feel worst.

Three weeks into my devastating news, I just could not keep it in anymore. I looked at my chapters that I had written before. I think I was on chapter nine at the time, when I wanted to give up writing. I did not have any desire to continue. One day, I was sitting in my office. I stood up and I walked out the door.

I had no idea where I was going. It seemed that God was leading my steps. He led me out the door and towards the PX. I kept my head down. Each step felt like I was running. When I approached the PX, I saw the PX manager. She was talking to her subordinates.

"Excuse me, but I need to talk to you." I yelled.

"Ok, come into my office." she said.

15

'How Percell got his groove back'

I know the title of this chapter is not original, (It's from a great movie called 'How Stella got her groove back') but it fits this story.

I was distraught over my wife's news of leaving me and getting pregnant with her new friend. I could not believe what was happening to me. I needed to find someone to talk. After three weeks searching, I found that person.

We spoke before on a few occasions. It turned out to be that she was from my hometown. She was attractive and short. I think she was 4 feet 11 inches tall. Her complexion was dark skinned and she wore her hair short. She looked similar to the rhythm and blues singer, Lauren Hill. Every time I saw her, a man was always in her face.

On this particular day she was talking to her subordinates. I walked towards her. She looked at me and could tell something was wrong and invited me into her office. As we walked in, I broke down crying. It was a rush of emotion that came over me. She asked me what happened, but I could not speak. She said "Come on; let's go to my room where you can have some privacy."

I know what you guys are thinking out there. Cry a little. Get some sympathy and then have sex. That did not happen at all. Yeah, that's right. It really did not happen!

As we walked to her room, I kept my head down the entire time. I still had tears in my eyes and I did not want anyone to see me. She opened the door and invited me to sit in a chair. She looked at me as if I were crazy. "Tell me what's wrong. What happened?" She asked.

I could barely talk. My mouth was dry. I was so embarrassed to be there. I pushed the words out of my mouth. "My wife is pregnant by her boyfriend. We were going to counseling. I was trying to make things work out. I am going to miss my son. I loved them so much, now things are different. This is the end of the world!" I said.

"This is the beginning of the end"

She listened to me while she was puffing on a cigarette. "This is the worst day of my life. I have lost a wife and a son. I care for them so much. Now it is all gone." I said. She looked at me and took a long pause. Then she told me something that has and always will stay with me for the rest of my life.

"This is the beginning of a new life," she said.

"What do you mean the beginning? I have lost everything. My wife and son are the two most important people in my life." I said.

"Yes I know. You cannot change the past; you must look to the future. Your son will always be there for you and because of him, you have to carry on your life," she explained. She also put the idea of getting my son to live with me.

We talked for about a half an hour and I began to feel better. As I was about to leave, she told me that I could talk to her anytime. I thanked her. I was about give her a hug when she said, "I would not try that if I were you." I paused and looked at her. I could tell that she meant business. I thanked her and left.

As I went back to work, I felt strange for telling some one I really did not know my business. I also felt embarrassed the way we departed. I was thankful that she listened to me.

I will refer to her as 'Misty'.

I saw Misty a few days later. She asked me if I was doing better. "If you want to talk, just let me know," she said. I did not jump at the opportunity; I told her I was doing ok.

A few weeks later, I thought I would stop by the PX and say hello. Misty was in her office and she invited me to come in. We talked about our hometown and my family. I asked her about hers. She told me that she was going through a divorce as well. Damn! Can anyone stay together?

This was her second and last marriage. She told me about her three kids. She had lived a very tough life. Her latest husband beat the living hell out of her. He consistently called her on her cell phone from Virginia to Kosovo.

According to her, he also tried to kill himself and is very jealous. He would yell at people who would look at his wife. He accused her of cheating on him. He punched holes in the walls at their house. He spent her money and drank heavily.

And my wife thinks I'm a bad person!

She told me that she volunteered to come to Kosovo, to get away from him. She told me that she was married to him for twelve years. While telling me her amazing story, she never cried.

And I thought I had problems!

She said that she has had enough of men. She did not want to marry again. I could see that she is a very strong willed woman.

After a month of talking to Misty, we became good friends. We had a lot in common. First, we were from the same area of Virginia. Secondly, she was a year older than I and we shared the same zodiac sign. Thirdly, she listened to me when I was on the radio in the eighties. And lastly and most importantly, we were coming out of bad relationships.

We were not looking for anyone, but yet we (or at least me) needed someone to talk to. We both enjoyed each other's company. It was really fun to be around her. I felt like I was in high school again!

She told me that she admired me from the very beginning. I never tried to come on to her, nor suggested sex. Our relationship or friendship was strictly legit.

This is when 'Percell got his groove back'. By now, everyone knew that we were good friends. Guys backed off and did not hang around her as much. It was if I was the luckiest guy in Pristina! There I was with one of the cutest women around, and to top it all off, it was real. Our relationship was real. Not planned. It felt so good being around her.

It was not all peaches and cream however.

There were some things that I did not like about her. She was a little unladylike. She spoke rather roughly and cursed a lot. She smoked and drank alcohol. At times she was a little argumentative. It seemed that she liked confrontation.

I assumed that because of her troubled past with her husband, this type of behavior was normal for her. Still through these episodes with her, it felt good that someone was somewhat interested in me.

My confidence was through the roof. My head was lifted high and it felt good to get my 'groove' back. I realized that I had lost my groove years ago and I forgot how good it felt.

Some nights I would go to her room and watch a movie. I would watch her fall asleep and think how many men would love to be in my shoes right now.

In the military, friends come and go and this wasn't any different. After getting to know 'Misty' and hanging out with her for a couple of months, it was time for her to leave Kosovo. She reassured me that my life would continue. She gave me confidence. She caught me when I was falling. She listened to me. She held me and wiped my tears. She held my hand and was my friend if only for a short time.

16

Meanwhile, back in Kosovo

It had been a month since my wife told me the terrible news of her pregnancy. I had called her twice. In our first conversation, she again apologized to me. In an interesting twist, she wanted us to get back together.

I guess she wanted me to act as if nothing had happened. I told her that our relationship was beyond repair. I told her that I could never trust her again and without trust, in my opinion, you cannot have love.

In our second conversation, I asked her when she was due. She dropped a bomb on me when she said around Christmas. That meant she conceived back in April, the first month she moved out of our apartment and my first month in Kosovo. She then informed me that after she had sexed 'Taki', she felt so terrible that she kicked him out. Because of that she thought it was acceptable that we get back together.

I was so disgusted with her; I really did not want to talk to her at that time. However, this is not the end of our story, as you will read later.

Friends

Since my arrival in Kosovo, I have met many people. The rest of this chapter is dedicated to Captain Todd, a man who I consider a real close friend.

Captain Todd, a Caucasian, is a native of Texas. He came to Pristina in April. He like the rest of us slept in the large green tent when we first arrived. While we were in the tent, others talked and he sat mostly quiet on his bed. In the following months I would see him around Film City.

The first time we got into a conversation was when we had our monthly birthday party. We always celebrated our service men and women that had birthdays in that particular month. We would sing happy birthday to them and make them a pre selected karaoke song to us.

The Red Cross provided all the birthday gifts. After the gifts were opened, the disco began with the electric slide. I have been doing the 'slide' for almost twenty years, so it is not hard to me. Captain Todd, on the other hand, had never seen this dance. He was on the dance floor moving uncoordinated in the wrong direction and bumping into people.

I 'slid' in to help him out. I said, "Hey Sir, slide this way. Now move that way." He wanted to learn so badly. He was trying with all of his might, but not quite getting the steps. I 'slid' with him for the next two songs, showing him how to do it correctly. He never really caught on. Exhausted, he took a break.

I found a dance partner and we did the 'electric slide' to perfection. The Captain watched us in amazement.

The next day he came to my office. He told me what a good time he had. He told me that he had a meeting at Camp Bonsteel in two weeks and was wondering if I could take him there.

Two weeks later, we made the trip. While driving to the camp we struck up a conversation. After talking to him for a few minutes, I could tell he was a down to earth person.

We talked about everything. I told him about my wife and my problems at home. He told me about his problems at home. We had a lot in common.

Soon, we began to go to Bondsteel just about every day. We would go to Bondsteel's dining facility and eat lunch. Then I would go on a supply run, pick up mail and then I would stop by the Red Cross and pick up our newspapers. We gelled together. I even have stories to tell, for example:

Captain Todd, the traffic and I

Driving to Camp Bondsteel normally takes about 45 minutes one way. The trip is always interesting. As I told you a few chapters ago, the roads were in terrible condition and filled with many potholes. You could not drive off the pavement; because the sides had not been cleared of land mines.

Now the roads are getting paved, which makes the trip more comfortable. That is not the problem. The problem is when two road construction men are trying to control the single lane of traffic while the roads are getting paved. They have neither rhyme nor reason as to how many cars they let pass before they stop traffic and let the other lane go through.

The one thing Kosovo has taught me is patience. You can't yell at them because they can't speak English, so you could sit in a vehicle and wait as long as fifteen minutes before we would move. On top of that, the Albanians don't have patience for waiting that long, so they try to fit two cars on a one-lane construction highway. Talk about your near head on collisions!

One day we were stopped at the construction site and waited almost ten minutes for the road crew person to wave us through. I looked to the rear of the vehicle to see if another car was trying to pass us. Captain Todd would get so angry with the other drivers for not waiting their turn. He would say,"Why can't these people just sit here and wait. Can't they see if they try to get in the other lane that the car from the other direction would have to stop?"

We were waiting our turn to pass by the construction site. I told Captain Todd that a car was heading over to my left to pass. He jumped out of the vehicle with his weapon in his hands and used it as a flag to signal the driver to get back in line. He looked like Tom Cruise (Sorry Tom) or some Hollywood actor. This was his method of solving the problem and it worked every time.

One time he got so pissed off at the Albanians trying to jump ahead in the line. He jumped out of the car as I was slowly moving forward. When he finally turned around, I must have been a mile up the road. He ran to catch up with me.

Some days we would travel to Bondsteel with another person. I would drive and Captain Todd would sit in the front seat. He and I would smile at each other when we would get close to the construction site. I would give him a nod and he would jump out of the van yelling and screaming at the people behind us. The person in our van would think that he was crazy!

Captain Todd, the traffic accident and I

One evening while returning from Bondsteel, we ran into another traffic jam. We sat there for a half of hour. The Captain said, "Let's see what the hold up is." Once we got out of the van, we saw a bunch of people standing outside their cars looking at an accident. At an intersection, there was a truck that was over turned and lying off of the road. However, we did not see any bodies.

For some reason nobody wanted to pass the truck that was overturned. It was a clear pass for cars to go by. This was the worst case of rubber necking I had ever seen. I asked, "What is the problem? Why are the cars not moving?" I quickly saw the problem.

There in the middle of the crossroad was a female Kosovo police officer. She was trying to direct traffic. She saw us and said, "Please help me." The Captain pulled his gun and started waving people in the direction of their cars.

It took us about fifteen minutes to get the first car to go in the right direction. I ran to our vehicle, got in and pick up the Captain where he was still directing traffic; he jumped in and the police officer took over.

Captain Todd, Albania and I

We supported five American officers posted in Albania. Because of the nine-hour distance by car, we flew in a Ukrainian helicopter nicknamed 'old shaky'. We flew to Duress, Albania, to give the officers mail, movies and sodas. A small finance team from Bondsteel went with us so the officers could cash checks.

When I stepped off the helicopter, it was the first time that I had seen palm trees! The post is located on the Adriatic Sea, seventy miles west of Italy. The NATO post is right on the beach. There is one problem; you cannot swim in the water. There are so many toxins and pollutants that will ruin your health.

One of the officers took Captain Todd and I on a quick tour of the city. That is a story within itself. The city is run down and war torn (and I thought Pristina was bad!) A few hours later, it was time for us to go. We boarded the chopper.

The Ukrainian pilot started the engine. 'Whoosh'! The helicopter made a noise from the engine. He started it again 'Whoosh, whoosh' as the engine tried to start. The co pilot told us to get out. The Ukrainian pilot started the engine again. 'Whoosh'. We saw a ball of fire that came out of the top of the chopper. Then the engine started. "This is normal," the co pilot said he encouraged us to get back on the chopper. Nobody said a word the entire trip back.

Captain Todd, the AFRICAN UNMIK and I

I have told you that the US UNMIK (police force) and I are close friends. One evening we got an invitation to attend a US UNMIK party that was held in downtown Pristina. What we did not know at the time was the US UNMIK and the African UNMIK had parties at the same location in separate dance halls.

The first dance hall we went to was playing techno music. There were only a few people there. I decided to check out the other dance hall.

When we walked in, we saw the biggest group of African UNMIKS (police) I had ever seen. They were playing traditional African music and singing in their native tongue.

Captain Todd asked me what they are singing. (Like I know!) I laughed and jokingly replied, "White man here. Dinner is served!" They turned out to be a good group of guys from all parts of Africa.

They invited us to go out on patrol with them for a few hours the next day. This was a great experience for us because we got an opportunity to see them in action. They also taught us how to use their radar gun.

Captain Todd, the movie and me

We did this only once and it was fun. Camp Bondsteel was showing the world premiere of *Mission Impossible Two*. The movie was not being shown in Pristina and we wanted to see it badly. We crept off post and went to Bondsteel. The movie started at 8:00 p.m. We got back to Pristina around midnight. Boy was I tired the next day!

For the rest of our rotation in Kosovo the Captain and I saw each other every day. We would always be up to 'no good'. We had so much fun in the four months that we were stationed together. No matter where we went. We share a lot of great memories; he was and still is my 'pal'.

17

Landshut or Landstuhl?

Let me tell you one of the funniest stories that happened to me since I had been deployed. As a matter of fact this story did not happen to me while in Kosovo. Allow me to explain:

I noticed that I was having a little vision problem while I was in Kosovo. If I keep my head straight and look to the extreme right my vision would double. If I move my head or turn my body slightly it would go away. I did not think it was serious. I don't know when it started, but it did bother me a little.

One day when I was at Camp Bondsteel, I decided to go to the optometrist. The doctor performed a battery of test. He knew what it was right away. He called it right eye palsy, but he wanted to confirm his thoughts, so he called another doctor in Ramstein, Germany. The doctor in Germany told him that he wanted to see me right away.

This made me a little nervous because I thought it was serious. The optometrist at Camp Bondsteel started to make all the necessary arrangements. He told me to be ready to leave Kosovo on Friday. I was to meet his medical evacuation (Medvac) staff around 1:00 p.m. on to fly back to Germany.

Friday came by quickly. I left Pristina for Bondsteel. I met the Medvac team. There was another Sergeant that was leaving with me. He had vertigo. We stood outside and the helicopter arrived. We flew on a Black hawk helicopter, one of the best helicopters the army has. We flew to Skopje, Macedonia within fifteen minutes. We then traveled by car to the airport. There were boarded on a military plane that was headed to Germany.

We arrived in Ramstein around 7:00 p.m. There was an assistant to the Ramstein hospital team that met us. He put our bags in the van and we drove to the hospital. He told me that my doctor would be seeing me tomorrow.

As we drove to the hospital there was a sign that read 'Landstuhl medical facility'. Landstuhl is a small town right next to Ramstein. It is a very quiet town in the valley. The hospital is located on the top of the hill looking into the city. We drove up to the hospital and got our room.

At 9:00 a.m., I met my doctor. His name was Dr. Birdsong. He preformed many tests on my eyes. It was 10:30 a.m. when he took a break to get a book off of his shelf.

He read a few pages and then turned to a chart. "Read this," he said. I repeated what I though the chart said. He looked back in the book. He took another book of the shelf. He then stood to my left side and told me to keep my head straight. He asked me if I could see him standing there. For a moment, I could not. Then I forced my self to concentrate. I saw two of him!

"Ah ha!" he said. Then he went to another book. He found more info. He informed me that I have a condition known as Left Superior Oblique Palsy. I asked what cause this condition. He said that I had a 'sleeping stroke'. One night when I slept, I had a mild stroke. That stoke constricted the left eye muscle. Thus, it rendered the motion of the eye muscle that moves to the right and to the extreme left.

The next day, I had a CAT scan done. The out come was negative. I had a blood sugar test. The test ranged from 60 (low) to 140 (high). My blood sugar was 84. I did not need glasses. So the doctor told me that in time my palsy may go away.

All of these tests were performed in a span of three days. Remember I flew into Germany on Friday; my first test was on Saturday. The rest of the tests were performed on Monday and Tuesday. My return flight to Kosovo was scheduled for Friday so I had a couple of days to kill. I decided to go to Stuttgart to visit my son.

I called a friend of mine from Stuttgart. He agreed to make the four-hour drive to the hospital and he picked me up.

Over next few days I spent time with my son. My wife was showing her pregnancy. By now we both knew the possibility of us getting back was not going to happen. We talked about divorce, but did not make any plans. I told that when I am finished with Kosovo, we would meet with a lawyer.

In the meantime the Bo and I had a great time together. We done all of the things we used to do. We hung out at the 'power zone' (electronic store); we ate at McDonalds and I visited some of my co-workers at my old place of employment.

While I was visiting my co-workers, I thought that I would save a few dollars and purchase a train ticket from the US military ticket office to get back to Landstuhl. I told the clerk that I needed a one-way ticket.

The next day, I arrived at the train terminal in Stuttgart. I was not running late so I had a few minutes on my hands. I walked around and bought an ice cream. I looked at my watch then I headed to the track and boarded the train. I looked over my itinerary. It read:

Place		Hour	Track
Stuttgart	ab (leaves)	18:55 (6:55 pm)	16
Munich	an (arrives)	21:12 (9:12 pm)	17
	ab (leaves)	21:28 (9:28 pm)	22
Landshut	ab (arrives)	22:18 (10:18 pm)	5

When the train departed, I took a nap.

When I woke up, I wrote notes on a pad of paper for this book. I think I was writing the first of the 'divorce' chapters. Anyway, I was sitting there watching the houses go by and jotting notes. It was nothing special. I caught another nap and soon it was time for me to get off the train in Munich.

A tad off course

I caught the next train and was heading toward my final destination of 'Landstuhl'. When the train stopped, I hopped off. I looked around. I did not notice any of the buildings. I thought I got off at the wrong city.

I looked at the city sign and it read; 'Landshut'. I looked at my ticket. It read 'Landshut'. Was I in the right city? I looked at the sign again. I looked at my ticket. I looked at the sign. I looked at the ticket. Back and forth my eyes travel from letter to letter and compared the writing on the sign to the ticket. Then it hit me. I had purchased a ticket to the wrong city. I was supposed to be in 'Landstuhl' and not in 'Landshut'. I am in the wrong city! I felt like I was in the 'twilight zone'.

I ran out of the train station. Panicked, I ran across the street. I saw a gas station. I ran in. I asked in broken German where I was. The attendant told me Landshut. I asked for a map of Germany, I wanted to see exactly where I was. There was another German there. He spoke to me in English. "What are you looking for," he asked. I guess he could tell from my face that I was in panic.

The attendant picked up a map and showed me where I was. My worst fear was realized. Not only was I in the wrong city but also I was on the other side of the country! I was not even close to where I needed to be. If you have never been to Germany, let me tell you how far off I was.

Let's pretend that we are in my hometown of Chesapeake, which is only 30 miles from the Atlantic Ocean. I needed to be in Washington, D.C. Instead, I am in Indianapolis, Indiana.

I looked at the map in disbelief. If you read my arrival schedule, I was supposed to arrive in Landshut at 22:18 p.m. or 10:10 p.m. Thursday evening. By the time I ran to the gas station and asked questions it was almost 10:45 p.m. I asked how long would it take for me to get to where I needed to be. One guy said it would be about an 8-hour drive by car or 600 miles away!

I needed to be in Ramstein at least by 9:00 a.m. in the morning to check out of the hospital and get a ride to the military airport. My flight was leaving around 11:00 a.m. Keep in mind that military flights times are flexable. If I were not there, I would be in big trouble.

Panic was on my face. The only thing I could think of was to go to the police department. I asked him to drive me to the police station. He told me that it was only a few streets down. I still could not believe where I was. I did not check the ticket for the correct name of the city. Landshut. Landstuhl. So damn close in spelling, boy, am I in trouble!

We arrived at the station and I flung the door open. Since the guy that drove me spoke fairly good English, he agreed to stay with me to translate in German. I told the police;

Me: "Help, I need to get to Ramstein!"

Police Officer: "Ok."

Me: "You don't understand, I am in the US Army! I am stationed in Stuttgart, but I am deployed to Kosovo."

Police Officer: "Ok."

Me: "You do not understand, I cannot miss the plane that will be taking me back to Kosovo tomorrow morning!!"

Police Officer: "Ok."

Me: "You don't understand, I bought this ticket and I need to go to Landstuhl. This ticket says 'Landshut'. I needed to go to Landstuhl, but this ticket says 'Landshut'."

Police Officer: "Ohhhhhh."

Me: "Now you understand??? How can I get there? Can you guys fly me there by helicopter?" (I was desperate.)

Police Officer: "No, I can't do that. Maybe you can rent a car?"

Me: "That will take all night!! Besides there isn't a place that is open."

Police Officer: "Ok."

Me: "Please. I need some help."

Police Officer: "I have a friend that drives a taxi."

Me: "A taxi?" (I thought that this man must be crazy! Is he suggesting that I drive to Landstuhl by taxi?)

Police Officer: "He can drive you to the next biggest city from here. That city is Munich."

Me: "Oh, yeah! That's right. If he can drive me there, I know I can get on a train and get back to where I needed to be. How much will he charge me?"

Police Officer: "Let me call him."

I waited in the room. He called his friend. They talked on the phone and he told him my problem. He was laughing on the phone.

Police Officer: "My friend will be here in five minutes. He will charge you 50 marks (30 dollars)."

"Ok", I said.

The police officer giggled to him self as he walked away. The man who drove me to the police station said that I should be able to catch the red eye train from there.

The taxi arrived. I thank the policeman for his help. As I walked out of the door, I told the man who gave me a ride to the station to write down his address. I told him that I would buy him a small gift from Kosovo. He gave me his address and we shook hands.

"Thanks for everything. I really appreciated what you have done for me." I said.

"No problem. I hope you make it. Have a nice flight back to Kosovo," he added.

I hopped in the taxi. As we wound through the small city, the taxi driver said, "Kosovo huh." "Yes," I said the word, 'Landshut'. He looked at me and said "Yes, Landstuhl!"

We drove on the autobahn. I saw a sign that said "Munich 180 KM". This meant we were about 100 miles away from the city. I looked at my watch; it was 11:15 p.m.!

I have been on the autobahn many, many times. I have traveled as fast as my little Honda Civic would go. I think the fastest speed I have driven was about 90 mph.

When we were on the autobahn, we were moving. We were in a Mercedes Benz taxi. I looked at the speedometer. We were going over 110 mph! Since I was in a Benz, it did not feel like we were going that fast. The car felt comfortable and we hugged the road. At the pace we were driving, we would be in Munich within an hour.

We arrived at the Munich train station at 12:10 a.m. I paid him the fifty marks and ran inside.

The first thing I noticed was there were no trains around. There was nobody to help me. Panic really started to set in. I looked for the information desk. There was a man standing behind the desk. He just had cut off the light and was about to leave. I ran towards him.

I told him about the wrong train that I took. I showed him my ticket. He acted like he did not want to help me. He looked at the ticket. He printed another ticket with a schedule and gave it to me. Because it was late, he did not charge me. He may have thought that it was an honest mistake.

He told me to go down two flights and he gave me the track number. He told me to hurry the last train was arriving in ten minutes.

I made it to the train. I looked at my ticket. I looked at my watch. It was going on 12:35 a.m. This train will arrive in Landstuhl at 07:35 a.m.

I made it back to the hospital. I got my bags and checked out. I caught a shuttle bus to the airport. Needless to say I was dog-tired. My military flight left on time.

As the flight reached its altitude, the person sitting next to me had no idea what my past 17 hours had been. As I closed my eyes, I told myself "this is one for the books."

18

"24/7, don't wanna go back"

The entire population of Kosovo lived under the fear of the Serbs. They had to deal with them 24 hours a day. 7 days a week. Since NATO's arrival things are getting back to normal; but the Albanians don't won to go back to their past.

I too, do not want to be reminded of the past.

Now when I called my wife, she goes on and on about how terrible of a husband I was. She always reminded me that we should have gone to counseling back in 1990. According to my wife, her past has been hell.

I really didn't want to hear about that stuff. I only wanted to hear the voice of the Bo. I missed him so much. During my short trips back to Germany, we got use to being around each other. Then I had to re deploy back to Kosovo and by doing this, it took something out of me. Although this was my fifth month deployed it felt like five years.

I have learned that everything went on between my wife and I was for a reason. I also started feeling better about myself. I had 'torn myself' up and down in the past two months. As I was writing this book, I found peace and solace. I keep on telling myself that I am not a bad guy.

During this point, I really didn't want to talk to my wife anymore. I did not want to hear about how bad of a person I was. I just wanted to talk to my son. I wish when I called, he would pick up the phone. Well, I really don't know why I am worried about talking to her. We rarely talked about anything when I did call. Even when we were on good terms, our conversations would be short. This how are a typical conversation went:

Her: "Hello?"
Me: "Hey, it's me."
Her: "Yes."
Me: "How are you doing?" (I tried to show concern)
Her: "Fine, how are you?"
Me: "I'm ok. Nothing really new, it's getting cool here."

(Believe it or not up until this point, I was still sending here these chapters!)

"Are you still getting the stories I am sending you?"

Her: "Yes. What are you planning to do with these stories?"

Me: "I may publish them. I have no idea."

Her: (No response)

Me: "Anyway, is the Bo there?"

Her: "Bo, Papa is on the phone."

That would be the extent of our conversation. I really had no 'rap' for her. Believe it or not, the more I was writing this book, the faster I got over her.

We worked everyday in Kosovo. There were no days off. 7 days a week almost 24 hours a day. It seemed that everyday is a Monday. I was feeling better about myself everyday and was looking forward to the next day. Each day is a small victory for me.

As the end of the summer was coming to a close, I thought more about going back to Stuttgart. Every American had a six-month rotation and my time is almost up.

I did not want to return to Stuttgart, with all the bad vibes between my wife and me. I also had to put up with my nosey neighbors. The job here was fairly easy and the money is not bad at all. Plus I am receiving a good experience over here.

If anybody knows me well, I am a planner. I like to have things pretty much planned out. I think the reason I have had the problems with this impending divorce is because it's something you cannot plan. It took me by surprise, and caught me totally off guard.

I was about to go back to Stuttgart. I would have about 11 months left until I return to the states for another assignment.

As I looked around Film City, the place had grown. 'Misty' took me out of my low point in life and now I am beginning to enjoy life.

'Top'

At the US NSE (National Support Element), I had been checking out the First Sergeant, SFC Blakeney. It appeared to me that his job was fairly easy. 'Hmmm', I said to myself, "I could stay here another six month rotation and take over his job when he leaves."

The First Sergeant (or some soldiers call this position 'Top') is the person that is the 'top' Non Commission Officer (NCO) in the company. He has or supposed to have the most knowledge in the company (or at least find the person that has the right answer).

His knowledge ranges from administration, supply, and finance, day to day operations of the NSE, physical fitness programs, health and the morale of soldiers. Along with that, the First Sergeant has to be a firm leader. He runs the company. He makes plans for any and all activities like holidays, monthly birthday bashes and meetings.

The First Sergeant ensures that if there is a family emergency, the soldier will fly home. He checks and sometimes writes the Non Commission Officer Evaluation Reports (NCOERS). He has to be a counselor, a teacher, and a mentor of younger soldiers. He sets the example. He works late night and early in the morning. He works closely with the company commander. 'Top' makes decisions and enforces the rules. He is wise by his age and has experience to fall back on. Next to God, he is the man.

In most army unit's the First Sergeant's rank is a Master Sergeant or an E-8. When you achieve that rank, some E8's have been in the army over 15 years. In this situation however, the NSE's 'First Sergeant' position is that of an E-7 or Sergeant First Class, which happens to be my rank.

'If I could be the First Sergeant here in Kosovo for 6 months, then this would look really good on my military records', as I thought to myself.

I realized that I did not have a wife or a job in Stuttgart. My son is there, but he is used to me being away. So many things ran through my mind.

Take the 'easy right' (staying here) over the 'hard wrong' (away from my son). It was a difficult choice. After much thought, I decided to stay here in Kosovo and tried to become the next first Sergeant."

I said to myself, "As of right now, I don't wanna go back."

19

"Steve Percell"

In past chapters I wrote about my love of music. 'Steve Percell' is back on the radio once again, this time entertaining the military soldiers along with the local population both Serbian and Albanian.

Just who is 'Steve Percell'? Allow me to introduce you to him.

In the fall of 1979, I was a senior at Great Bridge High school in Chesapeake. I did not have any plans as to what I would be doing after graduation.

My father assumed that I was going to be a part of his business. As I have said, he was an electrician. He suggested that I should work with him after school. I did this for a period of time. The money was ok, but making a living out of getting shocked was not my thing. Also my fathers' short assed temper, made working with him worst.

WFOS FM 90

My high school guidance counselor was Mrs. Myers. She wanted to know what I would be doing after graduation. I told her that I would get a job somewhere. The following week, I saw her again. She asked me did I give any more thought about my graduation plans. I still had no true answer for her. Then she made a suggestion that has changed my life.

"You know, you have such a wonderful sounding voice." Mrs. Myers said. I was a little shocked. I had no idea where she was coming from. For a split second, I thought that she was flirting with me.

"What do you mean?" I asked. "You have a great voice. You should try out for the radio station at the technical school. The school teaches every one a trade like mechanics, cooking, farming, and clothing design and radio broadcasting. If you sign up, the classes are two hours everyday. The bus will take you along with other students to the technical school."

My eyes lit up. I never thought about broadcasting on the radio. I told her that I would check into it. "No," she said, "I will make the call and sign you up for the class."

It was all set in a matter of two days. I went to high school in the mornings and went to the Chesapeake Technical School in the afternoons.

The first day in the broadcasting class, we met our teacher. He was a big, rotund, silvered hair man named Jack Garrison.

We had about twenty people in the class and the first few months were very boring. We did not talk about what to say on the radio, or how to read commercials ('spots' as they are called in the biz). We spent long dry days talking about theories and technical jargon. We talked about how sound is made and how far it travels. We also learned about frequency and bandwidth.

This sounds so interesting to me these days because that part of broadcasting is good to know if you want to own a radio station. At that time we wanted to be on the radio. We wanted to be the next big time radio announcer like 'Wolf Man Jack, or Frankie 'The Chief Rocker' Crocker, or 'Daddy' Jack Holmes.

Mr. Garrison loved to talk. He would talk about his younger days. He would tell us stories of him in the 'war'. He claimed to have been a fighter pilot.

One of my favorite stories he told went something like this:

He'd say, "I remember when I was in the war. (He never told us which war.) I was a fighter pilot. One day I was flying high in the air. I was attacking the enemy. I must have shot down three planes. Then all of a sudden, there was a loud bang. The enemy shot back at me. I was heading straight down. My plane was in a stall. I could not pull out of it. I was heading towards the ground. The plane's engine was smoking. I did not want to jump out, because there were civilians down there."

He had out attention. We were hanging on every word! All out a sudden, he stopped his story as the class bell rang. We asked him what happened. "Did you jump out?" we asked. He stood there while puffing on his pipe. "Well, there were many options I had and I used the right one." he said. We asked which one he chose. He never told us. After the class, we came to the conclusion that he made up the story.

It was in the middle of the first semester and none of us had uttered one word on the radio. We would see the other students (second year students) on the radio. I was a senior so I started to doubt that I would ever make it on the radio.

As the semester wore on, Mr. Garrison started to pick students for the newscast and DJ positions. For our tryout, we had to read a prepared newscast. I looked at mine. I had never seen such big words, and it was a little over my head. I bombed my first audition.

Most of us could not pronounce certain words. Most black kids spoke in slang, or cut off the words. Instead of saying 'four' some would say 'fo'. Mr. Garrison always told us to enunciate the words. He'll say, "You are not back on the block. When competing for a real radio job, you will be hired to sound professional."

For some reason Mr. Garrison took to me. One day he asked me to read the news in front of the classroom. I stood up and read it. He took a puff on his pipe and said,"read it again."

After reading the news, he looked at me. Then he told me to stand near the wall. He told me to turn around and face the wall. My face was a few feet from it. I thought that I was being punished for something I had done. He told me to read the news again while facing the wall. I heard the kids laughing at me. I was so embarrassed. With tears running down my face, I read it again.

After I read the news, Mr. Garrison walked up to me and said that my voice sounded good but he wanted me to read from my chest and not my throat. He worked with me for weeks. Soon my voice would bounce off the wall and hit him squarely in the chest. "Now you are ready to be on the radio." he said.

It was January 5, 1980. I started broadcasting from WFOS FM 90.5. I became the first black DJ in the station's history. My show was only twenty-five minutes long with a five-minute newscast. When I got home I told my parents that I was on the radio. The next day my father and mother skipped work and listened to me.

When I got home from that show, my house was full of my relatives. My aunts and my uncles were there. They heard the show and were very proud of me.

I continued to work for twenty-five minutes on the air for the rest of the semester. After my show, Mike Lowery came on after me. He was a tall thin white kid that was also a senior at Great Bridge High School. Because he was a second year student at the station he had an hour-long show. He sounded great on the radio. I began to hang around him and watch how he 'spun' records. He made everything look so easy and had a great command of the English language.

WNOR AM 1230

Soon, he took me under his wing and for the next two months he really worked with me on my diction and enunciation. I wanted to know everything he knew about broadcasting. He taught and guided me.

It was June and we graduated from high school. By this time, Mike and I were talking about radio broadcasting everyday. One day he asked me if I wanted a tour of a professional radio station. Of course I said yes.

Mike told me that he worked part time at FM 99 WNOR. WNOR actually had two radio stations there. WNOR-AM 1230 played Rhythm and Blues, Top Forty and Disco. FM-99 played Classic and Album Oriented Rock (AOR).

On Friday afternoon, Mike took me to the station. I walked around in amazement. I met the personalities that I listened to on the radio. I loved it there.

I also met the many people that worked behind the scenes. I met the managers, directors, secretaries and the people that make the commercials.

As my tour was coming to an end, Mike pointed to the program manager of the AM Station. A man named 'Frenchie B' held this position. He was the supervisor of the radio announcers. When we walked by his office, Frenchie B was on the phone.

He was yelling at someone on the phone. When his call ended, he called us into the office. When we walked in, I could tell he was upset.

"Here is a friend of mine from the high school radio station," as Mike introduced me. "Hello, Mr. B. My name is Percell and I listen to your radio station all the time." I said.

"Hello. Nice meeting you." Frenchie B said. Then we walked out of his office.

We continued our tour. I walked down the hallway looking at the gold records the radio station received. I saw albums from The Jackson Five, Quincy Jones, Cameo and of course my favorite group, Earth, Wind and Fire. Mike asked me if I was ready to leave. I wasn't ready; this place was heaven to me.

All of a sudden Frenchie B called Mike in his office. A few minutes later Mike called me into the office. Frenchie B was sitting in his chair and asked me did I need a job.

I was in shock! "Do you mean working at the radio station?" I asked. "Yes, but there is one catch, you will have to start tonight at midnight and work until 6 a.m. Can you do that?" he asked. "Yes, I can be here." I said.

Frenchie B added, "Mike will teach you everything you need to know. If it works out you will work on the weekends. The pay is minimum wage and you will get the experience."

He walked out and returned with an application. I filled it out. I could not believe it! I got a job without interviewing for it. He asked me what my 'radio name' was. I did not have one, so I told him my real name, Percell Artis.

"Percell Artis?" he asked. "You need a name that is smooth and cool. Your name is a little unusual. Come up with something different. I will return in 10 minutes to get your application and your radio name. I need it to start promoting you and your show tonight," he said.

I tried to come up with a radio name, but I was so excited I could not think. I needed to calm down, so I called my mother and told her the news. She was so proud of me. I hung up the phone. Mike handed me an application and I started to fill it out.

I still needed a name. On occasion, some people thought that my first name (Percell) was my last name. So I used my first name as my last.

I thought about a simple first name. Dave or Joe but they really sounded corny to me.

I looked in the newspaper for some ideas. The first name I saw in the newspaper was 'Steve'. "That's it!" I shouted, "Steve" Percell. That is how I got my 'radio name'.

In the summer of 1980, I went to work at WNOR-AM 1230 on the weekends.

Once 'Steve' Percell began broadcasting on the radio, my fathers' feelings were hurt. After all, I was named after him.

My mother told me that she always wanted me to go to college. Initially, I did not want to go. As a teacher in the Chesapeake school system for over twenty years, my mother wanted to retire the year I graduated from college. That was her dream and I didn't want to disappoint her. I gave in.

WNSB FM 91.1

I wanted to keep my job with the radio station; I was getting some airtime and did not want to give that up. I sought to go to college in the same city I was working in. After narrowing my choices of two schools, I decided to go to Norfolk State University and major in Mass Communications.

I went to Norfolk State in the fall of 1980. Since I had experience in broadcasting from WNOR and WFOS, once again, a small piece of history happened to me. I was the first student ever to begin broadcasting as a first semester freshman on their radio station WNSB-FM Jazz 91.

WNSB's format was jazz. I worked Monday through Friday from 4:00 p.m. until 7:00 p.m. I was the 'drive time' announcer in the evenings.

I continued to work at WNSB-FM Jazz 91 through out my college years and worked at WNOR-AM 1230 Saturday and Sunday from my new time of 12:00 p.m. until 6:00 p.m. I did this for four years straight and graduated on time. That summer, my mother retired from teaching.

Steve Percell became a household name in my area. If you remembered 'Misty', she listened to me during my 'popular' years on the radio.

I stayed at WNOR another year after graduation from college.. I was only making $3.35 per hour there. In 1985, WNOR changed their format and began playing music of the '60s.

I went to work for a television station, WTVZ-Ch 33 (Fox) right up the street from WNOR. I worked in the film-editing department and was making $3.50 an hour. After working at the station for a year, I joined the army.

WLUR-FM

I had not been on the radio for years until I was stationed at Virginia Military Institute. The year was 1998. Although I was on for only nine months, 'Steve Percell' was back on the air at WLUR-FM. I played jazz and R & B. Believe it or not, I even hosted a pro wrestling talk show during that time. That show was so popular that I was on the radio and on local Public access TV!

RADIO KFOR

It was time for me to leave the states and I ended up in Stuttgart, Germany and you know the rest of the story. What you don't know is how I got back on the radio here in Pristina.

When I arrived at Film City, I bought a small radio. I was hoping to get AFN (Armed Forces Network). On that station, I could get the national news and music. After a week of turning the dial to both AM and FM stations, I could not find AFN. Instead, I found a station that played 'American music' and they spoke in a different language.

One day, I met Sergeant Jackson. He worked in the PSYOPS section. PSY-OPS means **PSY**chological **OP**erations. It basically means that PSYOPS (can) could influence the way Albanians think with the printing of newspapers, TV ads and radio. The section has a direct effect on how the Albanians feel about NATO. When the section prints a magazine with stories of what KFOR soldiers do, they make sure it's told fairly.

Getting back to Sergeant Jackson, he actually worked for KFOR magazine. He organized the entire magazine. He took photos, chose the color for backgrounds, and edited some stories and so on. As he gave me a tour of his office, he mentioned that they were also responsible for the radio station that they had here.

You know my eyes lit up! I asked him about the station. He told me he could show it to me later in the day. I asked where the station was located. He told me right by the front gate of Film City!

I met him later that day. We walked to the station. There was a small building with two rooms. One side was the production room where they made promos and commercials. Also this is the room where they gather news articles. On the other side was the radio station. It was very small. There was an old production board, the kind of board where I learned my broadcasting skills at the old high school radio station.

A computer played most of the music, so it was a very simple operation. I asked who was in charge of the station. You know I wanted to be part of the broadcast! I was introduced to an American officer, Major Tucker and his Belgium assistant Nina. I knew Major Tucker from picking up his mail, but I never knew he was in charge of the station. I reintroduce myself as the former 'Steve Percell' with many years of broadcasting experience etc, etc.

Right off the bat, I found that there were no soldiers on the air. It was strictly for the local Albanians. They were getting a salary and also getting a university credit. As my heart sank, I knew that it was impossible to be a part of the on air team. I was asked to give the younger kids any advice on the things I learned from broadcasting.

When I spoke to the Albanian broadcasting students, I was surprised that many of the students spoke and understood English. I taught them what I learned from the states.

A month passed by and I asked again if I could have a show for one night for one hour. Major Tucker told me that in the fall the radio station would change their name and it might be possible to obtain an on air slot.

"It's not about us, it's about the music"

I could not wait until the fall, so I asked again within a week. "You really want to be on the air don't you?" Major Tucker asked. "It's not that I don't want you to be on, but we have to be very careful of who we let on the air. We don't want to offend anyone. Of course you will be speaking English. Some of the population has a basic understanding of the language. It may be too hard for them to understand you." he said.

I could see Major Tucker was thinking. He continued, "I have a German boss. Maybe if you could write a proposal and the songs you will play and the length of the show, he may give you a try. He may listen to you."

You may remember, I told you that I met Captain Burton when I first deployed. We hit it off right from the start. He was a part time club DJ in Germany. For some reason he brought most of his CD's and DJ equipment with him. (He played music on many of our birthday bashes.) I did not bring many CD's with me, so I asked him would he like to be part of my show. He told me that he had never been on the air. I told him that I could teach him. He agreed, and we wrote our proposal.

Since Major Tucker brought it to my attention that most Albanians understood basic English, I came up with our 'famous end line' At the end of our proposal, I wrote, 'remember, it's not about us, it's about the music'. Needless to say they love it and agreed too give us a one shot deal on the radio.

"Friday night at ten o'clock"

I told everyone that I met to listen to the radio on Friday night at ten o' clock. I knew if I could get the word around, the better my chances were to being successful.

Friday night came around and I was nervous. It reminded me of my first time begin on the air back in 1977. To make a long story short, it was a success! Most people came up to me the next day and told me how much they liked the show because it was different.

Our show played a lot of 'old school' seventy and eighties, rhythm and blues songs. It was the same music that I used to play when I was on the radio, back in the day. As the show ended, I used that line that I wrote in the proposal, 'it's not about us, it's about the music'. Our show was accepted.

It felt good to be back on the radio and Steve Percell is alive again. The radio station did change its name in the fall to 'Radio KFOR FM 103'.

A month after our show began, Captain Burton returned to Germany, so I did the show all by myself. On occasions, I invited some of my friends to stop by and they got a chance to play a couple of their favorite songs. One of the people that I invited to play his music was John.

John was my Sergeant Major in Kosovo. A decorated veteran, I have nothing but the utmost respect for him. By coincidence, he was also stationed with me at VMI.

As I have mentioned before, I had a local weekend radio program on WLUR-FM. John listened to me while I was on the radio. He would call in a few times to try and guess my 'question of the day' promo to win a free pizza.

Now some five years later, there we were playing good music and talking about the good old times at VMI. 'It's like déjà vu all over again'.

I always had a theme on Friday night. On any given show I may have an all female vocalist show or an all male vocalist program. One night I had a 'quiet storm' (soft music) show, and then I followed that up with a funk and old school rap show. As you may have guessed, one night I had an all-jazz night.

I think the show that put me on the 'map' was my 'Soul Train' show. I bought a three CD set of 'Soul Train' (the old TV show) in the PX and played it that following Friday night. It seemed that every one in Pristina heard that show and called in weeks after that show aired. That really put me over the top.

The show took off and it was lengthen by another hour. I must say it was fun to be back on the radio. The radio station took a poll, to find out just how the new radio format was doing along with its most popular shows and DJ's. Keep in mind that I am the only English-speaker announcer/solider on the air. Also keep in mind that I am only on Friday night at 10:00 p.m.–12:00 a.m.

When the survey was finished, don't you know I placed 3rd overall in best announcer in all radio stations in two countries (Kosovo and Macedonia)? Not bad, not bad at all!

The show was very popular. I always said (as a joke) on the air that 'I am the number one radio program in all of the Balkans'. I know it is not true, but hey, I had fun with it.

Remember 'it's not about *us* (United States), it's about the music', that's important.

Peace!

20

'My friends are leaving me'

My radio life was great. My military life wasn't bad either. Film City's living conditions improved greatly and living here wasn't that bad. This led me come up with two good reasons for staying; which are:

Job Title: The chance of taking over as First Sergeant would be an excellent move on my part. This could lead to a future promotion.

The second reason:

I had nowhere to go: I did not want to go home to stare at four walls. My son was staying at his mothers' house. I missed him and wanted to go back home. However, in the back of my mind, I wanted him to stay with me when I returned to the states in June of 2001. I also realized that it might take bit of money to support him as well as myself. The bottom line was to make a little more money, put it in the bank and don't spend too much of it.

My plan was set. It needed to be put in action. I called my unit in Stuttgart and informed them of my plans. Actually, my Sergeant Major (E-9) told me the only way that I could stay if I got approval from a higher level.

As if luck was on my side, Major General Bowra (that is a two star general) was our US Commander in Film City. One day out of the blue, he walked into my office. I jumped to the position of attention. He told me to relax. I saw my opening; ask him if I could stay.

Me: "Sir, can I help you?"

MG Bowra: "No, just looking around. How is it going?"

Me: "Fine, Sir."

I saw my chance to ask him about staying another six months.

Me: "Sir, may I ask a question?"

MG Bowra: "Sure, what is it?"

Me: "Sir, (at this point I told him I was excess in my unit, what a great American I was and then I hit him with *the* question.) Can I stay an additional six months to be the First Sergeant?"

MG Bowra: "I don't see why not. Have you asked your Company Commander?"

Me: (Damn, I forgot to ask her, but I don't think she would mind, so let's go with it.) "Sir, I have told her that I am getting paperwork done to extend, and she doesn't have a problem with it."

Then I went on about what a great American I was (again).

MG Bowra: "Ok, if she signs the administration paperwork, then I will approve it."

I was in! I saw my company commander, CPT Jung, later that day and officially asked her if I could be her next First Sergeant. Then I went on about what a great American I was. She agreed and she signed my paperwork.

I sent the paper work up to the General and he signed it the next day. Then I had to forward copies not only to my unit in Stuttgart but at the army headquarters office in Heidelberg, Germany.

Some of my friends began to leave Kosovo.

My best friend CPT Todd left. I'll never forget the day he left. I saw him outside of his barracks smiling with his pearly white teeth and looking like Tom Cruise. He told me to come into his room. He gave me a small microwave oven. I wanted to give him a few bucks for the oven, but he said some one else left it for him when he first arrived.

"Misty" left. If you remember a few chapters back, she gave me my groove back.

CPT Burton left. He was the one that helped me get started as the 'number one' radio program in the Balkans area.

CPT Williams left. He was a big fan of the show.

Lieutenant Colonel Moore left. He was in my fraternity (Alpha Phi Alpha). He also supported the show.

SGT Beverley and SPC Carlsen left. These guys were a part of the NSE family. We worked together all day and into the night.

SPC Bethea left. He was my supply clerk.

SSG Brown who was from Virginia left. She was my favorite dance partner.

SSG Penn and SFC Grey left. SSG Penn and I love to talk about wrestling. SFC Grey just loved talking.

SFC Edwards left. Boy, this was some ping-pong player! There were many nights that we battled each other on the table. Through out our tour, we played fifty games he won 26 and I won 24.

MSG Zaborac left. He was a big, tall Texan. His wife sent him a 'goodie box' at least once every three weeks. And he would share them with everyone. He was famous around the camp for his homemade 'Rotal' cheese dip.

SSG Herrera, SSGT Shumate and SPC Barfield left. Although they worked at Camp Bondsteel, they were a part of out unit. On our mail runs we would go to their office and read our email.

Wendy at Camp Bondsteel's Red Cross left. She was a good friend. Not only did she provide us with the newspapers but also gave us boxes of microwave popcorn, soda and ice ceam. She also gave us gifts for our birthday bashes. She was also from Virginia.

SSG Clifton and SGT Jackson left. These guys told me about the radio station that was on Film City.

SFC Blakeney left. Well, he had to. I was taking his place as the First Sergeant.

There were many more people that I might have forgotten to list. If you are reading this and you were stationed with me at this time, please forgive me. We all had a great time (at least I did).

My fondest memories of the rotation were many. From the birthday bashes to the 4th of July to the cookouts to traveling throughout Pristina were great.

21

'First Sergeant Artis'

It was in the middle of October when I finally went on 'leave'. Or in other words, I took a break from being deployed. CPT Jung suggested that I should go home before I take on another six-month tour this time as the First Sergeant. I traveled back to Germany again.

Before I left Kosovo, I decided to give her a call to let her know that I was coming only to pick up our son. We talked for a bit and I told her I would be there in a couple of days. There was no real conversation. She said 'ok'.

I made the long trip to Stuttgart. I opened the door and ran in. I did not want my neighbors to know that I was back, so I kept a low profile. Again I walked around the house with little or no lights. I knew some people were chomping on the bit to find out not only 'how is Kosovo?' but also 'how are things, really?'

I was not up to the scrutiny. I did not feel like being on 'CNN', so I left my house early in the morning and came back late at night. All I wanted to do was to see my son.

I called my wife to tell her that I was on my way to their house. I was excited to see the Bo. I rang the doorbell. Her apartment had recently installed an intercom. The Bo asked who it was and I told him it was I. He buzzed me in and I climbed the stairs. There he was, standing there with a full head of hair, taller than what I remembered, with a big smile.

He said, "Hello papa!"

Me: "Hey, Bo!"

We hugged and he let me into the house. I saw my wife. Her pregnancy was in full effect. She was showing. She walked slowly towards the kitchen. She asked me if I wanted anything thing to drink. A couple of minutes passed by and she returned to where the Bo and I were standing. She looked at me.

"Looks like you loss some weight." she responded.

"Yeah, that happens when you are deployed." I said.

She invited me to sit down on the couch. She sat by the window, peering out of it. To me she looked embarrassed to be sitting there. With all that has gone on between us, here we are sitting there as if we were strangers.

We caught up a bit on what was new. Then the Bo took me in his room. He gave me the biggest surprise I have had in a long time.

He was reading!

That brought tears to my eyes. I don't know why. I was so surprised to see and hear him read.

"Bo! I did not know you could read. When did you learn?" I asked.

"I learned in school. I wanted to surprise you. I can also add and subtract too. Do you want to see?" he asked.

"Sure, let's see what you can do." I said.

We spent the next twenty minutes in his room as he was showing me his school projects and drawing. I was so proud of him. They really do grow fast.

The Bo stayed at my house for the next two days. We hung out and did the stuff that we always did. We would run and play at his old playground near my apartment. We raced to see who was the fastest. It was always one of his favorite games. We would go to the PX, watch movies and eat fast foods.

The last night before I was to leave Stuttgart, I dropped off the Bo at my wife's place. I told her that I was staying in Kosovo for another six months. She replied that I must like it there if I wanted to stay longer. I did tell her that I wanted to be away from her.

Her attitude was melancholy, somewhat in a reflective state. One time she was staring at the floor. I asked her what she was thinking. Her reply was 'the future'.

I quickly told her that when my deployment is done we would discuss the matter of our impending divorce. She agreed. I told the Bo, that I was leaving and I would see him in the springtime. He did not show any emotion. He was used to me being away from home.

As soon as her door closed I said to myself, 'As soon as this deployment is over. The Bo will live with me.'

I arrived back in Kosovo, ready for my new job. I knew Film City like the back of my hand. The place is fairly small and by doing the job as the supply sergeant became routine. I had built up a good working relationship with many people on post. I hoped the job, as first sergeant, would go well for me. SFC Blakeney made the job looked easy.

It didn't take long for me to get filled in on his daily duties. Most of his job was 'on the job training'. I had a good staff of people working in the building and

I had a couple of Sergeant Majors (E-9) to tap into their brain for any information.

SFC Blakeney hung around for two weeks. My replacement in the supply room came in doing this time. I was working two jobs at once. I was learning the ropes as the first sergeant and teaching the new supply sergeant his duties.

My new supply sergeant was a big Samoan, named Sergeant Ane. We traveled to Macedonia and Albania to show him where our property was located.

The following week, I found myself without much to do. SGT Ane was in my old supply office and SFC Blakeney was in my new one. I asked CPT Jung if I could go to Macedonia for a day or so. She said yes.

I stayed there for one night and I caught the shuttle bus back to Pristina. One my return trip back to Kosovo I met some one. Could it be? Have I found my groove again?

22

'The groove, part 2'

I have to back up a few months to fill you guys in for my next story. Remember CPT Todd? He was one of my best pals in Kosovo and we were always up to no good. I want to tell you one of the things we did that have a bearing on a particular person that has affected me till this very day.

During the summertime, the Shoe Factory was planning a huge block party. All NATO countries were invited to participate. The organizer of the show wanted participating nations to do their countries' most popular dances. For an example, the Turkish would do a dance from Turkey; the polish would do their native dance and so on.

The Americans were going to do a 'line' dance. That line dance was going to be the 'electric slide'. You may remember this was the dance I was trying to teach CPT Todd that dance a few chapters back.

Since the Shoe Factory doesn't have that many Americans that are assigned there, the organizer asked if Film City could send some US personnel down and join in.

When I first heard the news, I did not want to drive two hours to an event that was only going to last (for me) about 5 minutes. CPT Todd heard the news he asked me if I wanted to go. He suggested that we could make a night of it. We could watch the other dances, and then we could go downtown and eat.

I told him that I did not want to drive. That day, I just got back from the mail run at Camp Bondsteel and I was tired.

He said the show did not start until 8:00 p.m. It was already 5:30 p.m. and he was bounding with energy. As he begged, I looked at him. Without saying a word we both ran to our rooms to get dress. I met him back at the NSE around 5:45 p.m. We asked other people if they wanted to go. We found no one that wanted to make the drive. He jumped in the van and said, "Let's go!"

He got behind the wheel and sped out of the parking lot. He was driving like a mad man. I told him that there was no rush. He looked at his watch and said,

"It's already ten till six. We just got enough time to make it." He was passing everything in sight. He was blowing his horn, driving like there was no tomorrow and looking like Tom Cruise.

We made it there with a half an hour to spare. We jumped out of the vehicle and ran to the big parking lot where the festivities were being held. After our ID cards were checked, we walked in. I noticed that this was no ordinary block party. The organizer of the show hired a production company in Macedonia for the stage, lights, music and cameras.

They had a TV crew that was filming the event. To the left of the huge stage were nine very large TV screens. These screens served as monitors so the crowd could see what was going on the stage. Often the TV crew would show people in the crowd. It was being broadcasted all over the Balkans. It was an impressive sight.

"Aren't you glad you came?" CPT Todd said to me. "Yes. It's pretty cool. I did not expect to see such a big set up." I replied.

The show started with greetings from the event organizer. He brought out a local group of kids that preformed a dance. Then the Turkish came on the stage. The Germans was next and they brought in one of their bands to perform. They played for about fifteen minutes. During this time most of the Americans were 'warming up' for the electric slide. Some of the guys were still getting the moves down when we were called up to the stage.

When our music played, we did the slide. We slid to the song 'Man, I feel like a woman'. Some people were moving the wrong way, but we had fun. After the slide was over, we hung around a little.

After the TV show was over, a local DJ played some music and people started to dance. CPT Todd saw some foreign women who were standing on the side of the stage. We went over and asked if they wanted to dance. They told us no.

After three songs played, we found no one to dance. I think we asked just about every woman we could find. They all told us no. Frustrated, I was ready to leave the event. The party was quickly turning dull to me.

I said, "See. See what I mean. This sucks! We drove down here in breakneck fashion to just stand here. We all did a crappy electric slide and now I can't enjoy myself because nobody wants to dance."

CPT Todd said, "Let's go downtown to get something to eat."

"Eat!" I said, "Eat. It's almost 10:00 p.m. and you want to get something to eat? I can't eat this late. I'll watch you eat."

"Levern"

During our exchange, I noticed a beautiful woman that was wearing a long brown dress. She walked by and said hello. I knew everyone at Film City and quickly assumed she was stationed at the Shoe Factory.

"Watch this." I told CPT Todd. I waited for her to come back by us. We stood near the entrance about five minutes. As she walked back towards the entrance I asked, "Excuse me. Would you like to dance?" She looked at me and said, "I will be back."

I assumed that she did not want to be bothered. She looked to be in a rush. Since I was stationed in Pristina and she was at the Shoe Factory, I felt that she was not interested.

"See man, let's go. This party is dead!" I said. (Hey! That rhymes.)

We went downtown. He ate and I watched. Since it was late, we drove back to the Shoe Factory. We made arrangements to stay overnight. We stayed in the same big open-aired room that I slept in the first night I arrived in the Balkans. The next morning, we drove back to Pristina. This was the end of the story.

Or was it?

Now, let's fast forward to the end of the last chapter. One day, I went to the Shoe Factory. On the way back I took the shuttle bus back to Pristina. I was jotting down notes for this very book. Then I became sleepy and took a nap. As we were nearing the end of the destination, I woke up. A voice from the back of the bus asked, "Did you enjoy your rest?"

As I looked around, I saw the same woman that blew past me at the block party at the Shoe Factory.

"Yes, thanks I did, but it wasn't long enough. You are stationed at the Shoe Factory. I remembered you from the block party." I said.

"I was busy running around. I came back to look for you but you had left." She answered.

I looked at her for a moment and said, "It seemed like you didn't have time for me, so I left. I knew you didn't know me, but I wanted to introduce myself."

"I know who you are. You are about to become the new First Sergeant." She said

"How do you know?" I asked.

"This place is small, word gets around," she said.

We held a small conversation as I formally introduced myself. We began to chat. I found out that she was coming to Pristina to do some small contracting jobs. She was planning to stay a night or two. I told her about myself. I told her about the book that I was writing, and the pain of what I was going through in my personal life. I don't know why I told a stranger about my personal life, however, it felt better talking about my pain and getting things off my chest.

"Taking over as the man in charge"

The next day, SFC Blakeney left. In a way, I wasn't ready to take over as First Sergeant. I didn't want to let CPT Jung down, but I knew that I needed to step up to the plate and be on my own. I took a deep breath and began as the First Sergeant. I was to be the man that will be in charge of the US NSE for the next six months.

He was not gone a good ten minuets when the phones started ringing off the hook. It seemed that everyone knew that Blakeney was gone and I was there and in charge. People were asking all sorts of questions. It seemed as though I was going through some sort of early'test'.

The phone never stopped ringing. There were calls from Camp Bondsteel, Albania, Film City and the Shoe Factory.

There were many calls from the Shoe Factory.

One day our new US Commander (MG) Major General Smith was in my office. He met with CPT Jung and me. MG Smith had taken over for MG Bowra. He was the General that made it possible for me to extend for another six months in Kosovo.

We were asking MG Smith some questions, when that darn phone began to ring.

Me: "First Sergeant"

The other voice: "Hello, First Sergeant. How are you?"

Me: I'm fine. I can't talk right now; the General is in my office. Call me back later."

As the General continued to speak, I wondered who called. My thoughts were racing to match the sound of the lovely voice on the other end. Then I came to the conclusion that it must have been one of Blakeney friends.

Later that night, the phone rang again.

Me: "NSE, First Sergeant."

The other voice: "Still busy?"

Me: "No, who is this?"

The other voice: "Do you have so many women calling you that you don't recognize my voice?"

Me: (Growing impatient) "This is SFC Artis. I...."

The other voice: "I know who you are. You can't remember our conversation on the bus?"

Me: "Oh, yeah, now I remember. How are you?"

Our conversation lasted for about a half an hour. She said that she enjoyed our chat on the bus. She also said she thought that I was a nice person with good manners. I gave my mom credit.

'Levern' and I hit it off instantly. We would talk a couple of times throughout the day. I couldn't believe that she would be interested in getting to know me. I never gave her any indications that I was interested in her.

One day, we talked about the 'block party' at the Shoe Factory. She said that I shouldn't have left early.

"You shouldn't have left. I wanted to talk to you. There was one guy that was getting on my nerves and I wanted to leave. When I walked around the corner you were gone." 'Levern' said.

"Yes, I guess that is my fault. Sometimes I get a little impatient." I concluded. 'Damn!' Just like my father I told myself.

As time went on 'Levern' and I talked nearly three times a day. We had gotten to know each other really well. I found out that she was divorced, (there is a lot of that going around!) with a grown child. When she spoke I could tell she was intelligent. She had a ton of knowledge and was very helpful in getting me to solve various personal problems.

She was a reservist in the Navy. Her real job, back in the states, was working at a law firm. She gave me some good advice about getting a divorce.

"Misty? She is done."

'Levern' had been stationed at the Shoe Factory since June and was due to leave around Thanksgiving. As her time was getting near, the closer we became. I told her everything. I told her about 'Misty'. As you know 'Misty' gave me my groove back and now I had grown a little confidence in myself.

When 'Misty' left in September, I asked her to do me a favor. She was going back to Virginia and lived only twenty minutes from my mother. I asked 'Misty' to call my mom just once. If my mother heard from someone else that I was doing ok, then it would ease her mind in worrying over me while I was deployed.

I gave her my email address, my mother's phone number and her address. In return 'Misty' gave me her email and a work number.

A few days later, I called my mother and told her about 'Misty'.

I waited a couple of weeks until I emailed her. I figured that she needed time to rest and spend time with her family. In the email, I thanked her in advance for calling my mom. I also thanked her for talking to me. The next day, when I checked my email, I had no response. I thought that she might have overlooked it. I resent the email.

The next day I checked again. Still I had no response. I waited another week, nothing.

I felt a used. I poured out my heart to her and told her everything. I thought to myself, 'what if she was just as crazy as her husband?

I called my mother and asked if she had heard from 'Misty'. My mother said that no one had contacted her. I waited another week and without any email response from 'Misty', I called my mom again. She told me 'Misty' had not called. I began to think that my mom thought I was crazy, making someone up.

Now I was pissed. I sent more emails. The only way I could talk to her was at work. Hell, I didn't know her work schedule, so trying to get in contact with her was 'hit or miss'.

Finally, after six weeks, I spoke to her while she was at work. Our conversation went like this:

Operator: "Serving the best customers in the world. This is Susan how may I direct your call?"

Me: "Misty', please."

Operator: "Hold on, sir."

Misty: "Hello, this is 'Misty', how may I help you?"

Me: "Hello, what's up? It's me Percell."

Misty: (Unexcited) "Hey how are you?"

Me: "I am ok. I really do...."

Misty: "Hold on. (Talking in the background) Ok. So what is new?"

Me: "Nothing much. The place is still the same. The weather is turning...."

Misty: "Wait a second. (No, that item can be found over there) Ok, I am sorry."

Me: "Like I was saying, I really do miss you. Have you seen my emails?"

Misty: "Yes, I read them, but I haven't had the time to respond to them."

Me: "Not even one?"

Misty: "Yeah, I have been real....hold on. (No, sir you can find that item in...)Ok, I am sorry, what were you saying?"

Me: "My mother, have you called yet?"

Misty: "No, I will this week, I promise."

Me: "Yeah. Right!"

Misty: "No, I have been busy. Getting the kids back in school and you know, my crazy husband is still in the house. Wait a sec. (Yes, we have those...) Ok. Can you call me back I am...

Me: "Yeah, I know you are busy. I will talk to you later."

I called a couple of more times but the conversation never got better. I began to think that I never meant that much to her. I felt cheap and used. She did email me a short letter once. In October, she sent me a birthday card. The next month I got a crushed box of candy from her without any note in it.

She never called my mom.

I owed a lot to 'Misty' but in reality, I was just a deployment thing. I guess her and her husband worked things out. I told myself that she was a thing of the past and now I must move on.

Getting back to 'Levern', we would spend night after night talking to each other on the phone. She would come to Film City and we would have dinner. While I enjoyed her company, I was a bit on the defensive side and did not want to jump into a long lasting relationship. After all, my wife really crushed me and I felt used when I thought about 'Misty'.

'Levern' returned to the states in November. I asked her the same thing as I asked 'Misty'. Could she call my mom and tell her I am doing ok?

I am very happy to report that not only has 'Levern' called my mom *many* times, but she had visited her (from Maryland!) as well. 'Levern' sent many 'goodie boxes' for me including videos, cards and letters. I loved her for that. I always had something to look forward to when the mail came.

I feel very lucky meeting 'Levern'. She did not let me down. Even if she had, I wouldn't care. She had done more for me in the little time that I had know her than **any** woman had done for me (including my wife) in the last twenty years. 'Levern' showed me that love did stretch across the oceans.

23

Holidays in Kosovo

Thanksgiving

Seven months into my tour, the holidays finally came. I left for the Shoe Factory by bus a day before Thanksgiving. Once there, I met the NCO who was in charge of the activities. They had a tournament (pool, foosball, and ping pong) in the day room and showed a movie and football game. At noon we invited other countries to share in the Thanksgiving meal.

Christmas

The NSE staff went 'all out' for this one event. We had a door decorating contest, a Christmas tournament (b-ball, ping pong, pool and foosball), a secret Santa game, and we gave away Christmas candy.

We also arranged for our PX to give away a first place prize for the best decorated door. We gave out medals for first, second, and third place for the tournaments. We had the secret Santa with a limit of twenty marks (about 12 dollars) per gift. We got a Santa suit from Camp Bondsteel and picked a 'Santa' to give out candy.

During the month of December we received a ton of mail! The mail was not only from friends and families of our soldiers, sailors, airmen and marines, but from people around the states. I had never seen so many Christmas cards in my life. I was so overwhelmed; I picked five cards and wrote them back.

I told them that I was thankful that they remembered us during the holidays and took the time in writing us. In the letter I explained what our mission was, how we were living and what it felt like being so far away from home. I sent the letters out the next day. I did not expect anything in return.

A few weeks later, I received a letter from Mike. He was one of the people I wrote thanking him for the Christmas card. In the letter he asked me if there was anything we needed. He told me that he worked for Disneyland and worked in the entertainment costuming division assigned to the Eureka parade.

He also wrote that he is in charge of a project called 'Operation Uplift'. This project sends postcards, stationary and other small items from the Disneyland Park.

I wrote him back and thanked him. I told him that it meant so much to me by sending his well wishes.

It did not stop there. He wrote back again, this time he sent playing cards and Disney stationary. He also gave me his email address. The next day I sent him an email thanking him. I told Mike that I had a seven year old son and one day I would like to come and meet him. He gave me a standing invitation. As of this writing we are still emailing each other.

You see, friends come from all over the world and I consider Mike a friend. I'd like to thank him, his wife Liz and all the other people that work in the park for sending us such wonderful items. Although I was in Kosovo, I felt a little bit of America close to me!

New Year

Our brand new gym had only been open for a few months and we planned to have our New Year bash there. We moved all of our gym equipment to one side of the building. We decorated the gym with more Christmas items topped off with a disco ball. The event was open to all nations on post. We had people dressed in togas, to include me. It was great fun.

Midnight came and everyone counted down. As the clock stuck midnight, everyone yelled happy New Year. I stepped outside to catch some fresh air and heard off in the distance gunfire...that's the way the Albanians celebrate New Year.

24

A baby is born also know as 'Little Africa'

Smack dab in the middle of the holidays, I stepped back and thought about all the significant events in my life up to this point. (Any person who has ever deployed will confirm that deployments offer more than ample time for some serious soul searching.)

My 'military' family and friends were doing great but my own personal family wasn't.

My mother never liked me being located outside the country. To her Kosovo seemed so far away. She wanted me home even if 'home' was in Germany. You would think that by now she would be used to the idea of her son serving in the Army all over the world.

With regards to my soon to be ex-wife, it was clear that we were going to end up divorced.

The Bo was so as-a-matter-of-fact when I talked to him on the phone that it was difficult for me to get a sense of how he really felt. I always asked him how he was doing and about school. Consistently he replied simply and offered very few details. Deep down inside I knew that he may grow up without me and I did not want that to happen. Since he was so young, I wondered if he really missed me. Did he really care? Did he understand what is happening? Is that African guy taking care of him? Is he playing with the Bo, as if to replace me?

I spoke to my soon to be ex wife a few months after she moved out of our apartment. She informed me that she was working part time in order to make extra money to pay her bills. She complained that the money was not that great and of how tired she was. According to her, it was tough working a part time job, taking care of the Bo, and also doing all the cleaning and housework.

After all we had been through, my initial thought was, 'Now that's a switch! She didn't want to work when we was together; did not even want to lift a hand to help me with the bills! Good, she is getting a taste of how it feels to work and support someone other than you. Serves her ass right.' I knew that she would not work for long and really didn't care how tired she was trying to make ends meet. She made her bed and now she had to lay in it.

I knew that the wild card in all of this was my son. Despite this, I wanted to help out financially but I never did. I simply could not see myself sending money that she could misuse for something other than the care of our son. I had to come up with a strong *alternate* plan.

When my soon to be ex wife and I talked on the phone our conversations was next to nothing. On the side, I would ask the Bo if his mother had any company. He never let me down.

"He wants to do what?"

During the holidays, I called to wish my soon to be ex wife and my son a Merry Christmas. When the phone rang, the Bo picked up. I was happy to hear his voice. I was telling him that we are having a white Christmas. I told him how much I missed him. He told me about his Christmas gifts and the food he ate. We talked on the phone for about ten minutes, which was long for us. Then I asked him where his mother was.

The Bo told me that she was in the hospital and had the baby. I was startled. I asked, "So, if mommy is in the hospital, who is taking care of you?"

I assumed he would say his grandparents.

Then the bombshell hit.

The Bo said "Mommy's boyfriend."

"Really!" I said. At this time I got a funny feeling in the pit of my stomach. I felt like I was sick. It wasn't the food that I had, I guess it was the situation of another man taking care of my son and I'm not divorce yet. Part of me wanted to be there taking care of him. Part of me wanted to stay in Kosovo. I was really mixed up. There was a long pause on the phone. The Bo broke the silence.

"He wants to talk to you," the Bo said.

"He wants to do what?" I screamed. I could not believe my ears. He wants to talk to me. The man that got my wife pregnant wants to talk to me! What in the world can this man say to me? There were many things that were on my mind. It rushed together. I thought to myself; 'this man has got to be crazy.' I should cuss him out. Then I thought I better not do that. The Bo is alone with him. I don't want him to get pissed at me then take it out on the Bo.

Well, this man has got to be brave. The very nerve of him, what could he possibly say to me?

I then realized that I should not be mad at him, I should really be mad at her.

"Hello?" The Bo said on the other end, "Here he is."

For some reason, I stood up as if I was in the same room he was in. My fist was clenched. I was a tad nervous. My heart raced. He picked up the phone.

"Hello?" His African voice sounded a little afraid. "I want to say that I am taking good care of your son. Don't worry he is a good boy. This whole situation is messed up. One day I would like to really talk to you in person. I really don't know what else to say."

I could not hear anymore. I guess he was babbling on and on in his African accent. Right then and there I knew my marriage was over.

I pushed a 'thank you' out of my mouth for taking care of my son. That was all I could say. There wasn't anything I could talk to him about. I wasn't going to ask 'how is the weather' or 'have you read any good books lately?' type of questions. He put the Bo back on the phone. I told him that I would call back next week.

That night I had a tough time going to sleep I tossed and turned. The next morning, I made an appointment to see the legal team at Camp Montheith.

I spoke with a legal specialist about my impending divorce. I explained all the details about my soon to be ex wife's affair and having someone else's child. Two days later, I had separation papers drawn up exactly the way I wanted them. I was to have custody of the Bo; with her having visitation and she would have/keep the furniture. I hoped that she would agree to my terms.

I called the next week. She sounded a little weak. I asked her how she was doing. I heard the cry of the baby. I was lost for words.

Me: "So, how are you doing?"

Her: "I'm fine. The birth went smoothly. It was better than the first."

Me: "What did you have?"

Her: "A girl. Her name is Christina."

Me: "Oh, I guess you can give her a nick name like 'Little Africa.'"

I shouldn't have said that. I guess when you just had a baby the female hormones are a little frayed.

She hung up on me.

I called back a few days later. I apologized for the 'Little Africa' remark. I told her that I had put the separation papers in the mail and I needed her to sign them. We spent minutes talking about options for the well being our son. We agreed to give this topic a longer conversation for another day. I still had three months left in Kosovo, and anything could happen. It was also time for me to be leaving Germany altogether. I did not tell her that the separation papers included that fact that I wanted sole custody of our son. It was time to pick myself up and make her pay. I wanted her to regret what she had done to me.

I wanted to get even. I wanted to show her that my life would go on *without her* taking care of my son. I wanted payback. I guess you could say that I wanted to make her very sorry for what she had done to me.

I was full of spite, full of revenge, full of anger and very bitter. I thought about my childhood when my father told me that I would not amount to anything in life. Now look at me, getting a divorce because my wife had an affair. I was faced with the possibility of losing my son to another guy. I swore that was not going to happen. If my father was still living, I could hear him say, "I told you that this marriage was not going to work. You are still a failure." I could see that look of disgust on his face.

I even thought about finding a woman that I could 'date' when I got back to Germany. After thinking about it clearly, it looked like I was trying to find a woman 'off the rebound'. That would be playing tit for tat and I'm too smart for that. Besides 'rebound' relationships never work out.

Still, I wanted her to feel badly about how I was treated. Maybe I had it coming? Were we really in love? Did we marry for the wrong reasons? Was I such a hothead? Damn, do I really need counseling? Damn, do I need to see a shrink?

With all of the thinking I done over and over, I finally came up with a long-range plan on getting my son's life and mine together. I'm goal oriented; so I set a goal of two years for having resolution.

By that time, my soon to be ex wife wouldn't matter to me and I would hope to be over her.

This time, I had to do it for me!

25

Finally leaving Kosovo

It was April 2001, and my long deployment is coming to an end. My three-year tour of Germany was also coming to an end. Looking back, my time in Germany went rather fast. With all the problems that I had, I mostly spent two-thirds of my tour away from Stuttgart.

I came up with a plan on how I was going to get custody of the Bo. Before I left Kosovo, my soon to be ex wife and I finally talked at great length on the phone about what we were going to do with our 'new' situation.

A single parent/Advantage me!

We talked briefly about money. We had been married for ten years and the only thing we had 'jointly' was our son. As I have written earlier, after our child was born, she did not work. Although we never spoken about money in great length during our marriage, I think my soon to be ex wife's grandmother left her some money.

We never had a joint account, not in savings nor in checking.

I bought all of the furniture. I don't want to paint a picture that everything I bought was new. That is not true. When we were married I used a lot of furniture that the military provided for us. By the time we got to Stuttgart, I did buy a few pieces, but they were not in good condition. She sold what pieces she could and pocketed the money. I did not care; after all, I was saving money in Kosovo and had plans on buying new items once I got to the states.

When my soon to be ex wife moved out, she incurred more bills. I believed at this point her grandmother's money was running out, and her boyfriend was not helping much.

We spoke a great deal about the Bo.

As you know, I deployed in April 2000. The Bo's school was located on the military base. After the school year was over, she moved out of our apartment.

Before the school season began, she looked at enrolling the Bo into the international school in Stuttgart (where they speak English). When she called the school, she found out that it would cost almost 600 dollars a month. I told her I could give her half, but since she quit her job to take care of her baby, that plan got scrapped fast.

In the fall she called the American school. The school's administration clerk informed her that there are some families that lived off post and have their child bused to school. The clerk also said that **as long as I was deployed**, the school would pick him up. She gave them her address. As luck would have it, there were two other families that lived close to her as well.

Here is a big advantage I had in my corner. Because I am the one that is in the army, when I leave Germany, The Bo cannot go to the American school! That means my soon to be ex wife cannot afford to put him in the international school. This also means that she cannot go on the military base, period!

I threw out more reasons as to why he should be living with me.

I think one of my soon to be ex wife's biggest mistakes was that she did not teach him any German. When he was born, I suggested that she talk to him in German and I would speak to him in English. It didn't happen. She thought that teaching him this way; would slow his learning ability and he would be placed a year behind his normal class. Of course we had an argument over that.

The Bo did not have a clue as to what was going on around him. Since his mom moved off the American base, he told me that when he watched TV, it would be in German. He did not understand everything. His mom would go to the base library to get American videos. (If you remember, that is how she met her boyfriend during one of those trips!)

With hindsight being 20/20, what a great way of learning German by letting him watch German TV!

I also brought up the fact the Bo did not have any friends his age. I reminded her of a situation that I saw when I was there.

One day the Bo and I went to the park where other children were playing. I told the Bo to go over them and play.

A few minutes went by when it became apparent that there was a communications problem. The Bo could not speak or understand German and the kids understood no English. This intimidated Bo who separated himself from the crowd and went to sit on an old dirt mound across the street from the apartment. He looked so alone, sad and pitiful.

Then she finally chimed in. She told me that the Bo had missed me. He wanted to play sports. Because of her newborn; she did not have too much time for him. She also said that it was 'my time' to spend with him since I was coming from my deployment. I had been away from him a total of sixteen months this time and numerous times because of field exercises in the past; I needed to be his father.

I also assumed the African boyfriend couldn't replace me. They just did not play the way we did when I was around.

I think the light came on in her mind. She realized that he would be better with me. She agreed with me.

Originally, I think she told him that he would be living in the states with me for a year. If he did not like it, he could come back to Germany. Ha!! That played right into my hands! I knew that once the Bo gets a taste of the American life, he would want to stay with me.

I made a promise to her that I would take him back to Germany for visits. She agreed. I had this stipulation put in our separation agreement.

With that major problem behind me, I faced the reality of becoming a single parent. I barely knew how to cook. What ever I faced in the future, I knew that I had to learn quickly. My soon to be ex wife told me the types of foods that he likes. I never forgot the time she said that he 'was a low maintenance kid that is very well mannered'.

It was doing this time; I thought about future plans and wanting to put them in effect. Before I deployed to Kosovo, one of my soon to be ex wife's biggest gripes was that we did not travel much. She wanted to spend time at or near a beach.

Before I left Kosovo, I called DA again. (Man, these guys really know my name by now!) I wanted to find out my next assignment. More than ever, I wanted to be stationed in Hawaii. I wanted to hear my branch manager say that I was going there. Then I was going to call my soon to be ex wife and tell her that the Bo and I were going to Hawaii. Without her! I wanted her to be so jealous! I needed this more than ever!

My manager told me that the Hawaii 'slots' were filled. My heart sank. I was so disappointed. She told me to give her a call in the next couple of days to get an assignment.

I called the following week and found out that I was going to Ft. Lewis, Washington. I was happy with that. At least I can be closer to Hawaii.

"To cruise or not to cruise"

I was to report at Ft. Lewis in late July or early August. I thought that I would treat myself to a nice vacation before I go. I wanted to travel to an exotic island.

So, I checked out the Internet. I have never been on a cruise before, so I started to inquire about cruising to the Caribbean.

I looked at two cruise lines. I could not make up my mind. It was so confusing. Cruise line A's rooms were priced differently as where your room was located. If you had a view of the ocean then I had to consider another price. On this cruise I had to tip the waiter for food and drinks after every meal. Cruise line A stopped in many places, but for only a short period of time.

Cruise line B was a 'family' cruise. If I wanted to be alone, I had to put up with the possibility of kids running around. This cruise only stopped once but had certain restrictions. Then I had to consider my flight to and from a port of debarkation.

One day I called my mother and asked for CI Travel in Chesapeake. I remembered that CI Travel was located near my old high school. She gave me the phone number. I called and spoke to Lisa and told her about the cruise confusions.

She suggested that I should do an all-inclusive trip. She said, "For one price, you pay for the airfare, hotel and all the food and the sodas you can drink. How about something romantic?" she asked. "I have the perfect place for you. The hotel chain is called 'Sandals' it is in Jamaica. I will book the finest room on the resort."

My mind was racing. My first thought that came in my mind was to take 'Levern'. After all, she was the most deserving person I could think of. I was so excited. I quickly came to an agreement to stay at the 'Royal Caribbean' in Montego Bay from June 28 to the 1st of July.

After I booked the flight, I remembered my soon to be ex wife use to tell me that she wanted to go to a nice beach some where in Hawaii. Well, I was not going to Hawaii, but Jamaica sounded better! Get this, I was going and she was not.

'Levern' had really been a friend of mind since we met back in September. When she left during the holidays, we talked on the phone everyday. She was so concern with me being over in Kosovo. I thought that it was a little strange, since she had been stationed there as well. I could talk to her about anything. I told her my fears of becoming a single parent. I felt close to her.

She visited my mom three times. My mom really took a shine to her. When I talked to my mom, she said that she was a good person. "I know what is good for you, and she is it," my mom said. Somehow a mother always knows what is good for their children.

The entire time I was deployed in Kosovo, my soon to be ex wife sent me **two** small packages in twelve months. Inside them were the things that the Bo had done in school. She never sent any 'goodie boxes' nor did she ask if I needed anything. I wasn't surprised; when I was in school at Ft. Lee, VA, she didn't send me a damn thing.

My new friend was different. She sent me 'goodie boxes', videotapes and food. She sent cards and emails. She was becoming the new lady in my life. I didn't want to mistake my new love for a 'rebound' from my soon to be ex wife. I clearly did not want to compare the two; I wanted my new friend to stand up on her own merit.

I booked the trip. I called 'Levern' and told her that I had a surprise. "I want to take you to Jamaica this summer, just you and me. My mother will take care of the Bo." I said.

She couldn't believe it. She asked me if this is what I wanted to do. I told her yes because of all the things she did for my mom and me. So, now my summer began to take shape. My new life, my new plan and the new me was coming into form.

Goodbye, radio show

Whenever I visit Chesapeake, I always checked out the places I have grown up, went to school, or where I used to work before I joined the army. I love to see my old friends or co-workers. It's a part of me; my little history. My last job I had before I joined the military (1986) was working at WTVZ-Channel 33 (FOX, Norfolk). The last time I went back to the station (2000) there was some people I had worked with that were still employed there.

I make sure I stop by the Mass Communications department at Norfolk State University. I love to see my past professors. I make a point to visit WNSB-FM 91.

I always make time to stop by to see my old high school station, WFOS-FM 90. I get a kick out of seeing how the place has grown. I am very happy that the people have not forgotten me.

On some trips, I traveled back to Virginia Military Institute. I enjoy talking to the young cadets. One day, they will lead our armed forces. I was lucky here as well; I had a radio program for about a year at WLUR-FM.

Getting back to Kosovo, I was the first American to have a show that broadcast to the Albanian and Serbian people. I know these people did not have a clue as to what I was saying on air, but it was still bittersweet leaving. The music that I played made a louder statement than I could ever say.

One Friday night I had a translator with me on the show. The phones were ringing off the hook. He told me that people requested me to be on the air full time. That meant so much to me.

I wanted to make my last show special. I took a voice recorder around Film City. I had people record 'goodbye promos'. I had an enormous response. Many of the Albanian kids that listened to my show spoke 'good' English and gave me a great send off. I recorded about twenty promos. One promo went like this:

Person: "I want to wish Steve Percell all the best in life. His show was the best on radio KFOR. He played good music. We will be sad to see you go.

Me: "Thanks. I am glad that you enjoyed my time on the radio."

Person: "I know you have been here a year. Do you think you will be back next year?"

Me: "No."

Person: "That's too bad. I met the Danish guy that will be taking over your show. He asked me what type of music I like. I told him the same music Steve Percell plays."

Me: "Really! What did he say?"

Person: "I can't stay such words over the radio! You will be missed!"

I really enjoyed being on the radio. It was my little escape from my problems at home. It was a break for me to play some music and invite people on my show. I told them if they wanted to be on the air, to bring in their favorite CDs and I would play a song or two over the radio.

I had so many guests on the program they were all amazing. My show wasn't about playing *my* type of music; I played all kinds. Country, Jazz, Rock, Easy Listening, Instrumental, Soul, Old School; it didn't matter. My show was their show.

Goodbye, my friends

One could imagine how many people I have met in the last year. I met many people and soldiers from all over the world. There is no way that I could mention their names. They made my time go by quickly. I will definitely miss my radio station family (Radio KFOR).

I cannot leave out my dear friends that worked at the PX. In the same breath, I can't forget the UNMIK, Red Cross, Brown and Root and the other civilians. Lastly, I will never forget the children of Kosovo.

The NSE family was leaving as well. On March 30th 2001, we had a farewell dinner. Our four star General (Smith) came by to wish us well. We sat around and talked for two hours. Near the end, CPT Jung and I gave out presents to our staff. We all had tears in our eyes. I said a few words and spoke about everyone on our staff. I thanked CPT Jung for letting me stay on to be her First Sergeant.

April 1ˢᵗ 2001, my replacement finally arrived. He was an American reservist living in Denmark. He spoke Danish fluently. He wore the rank of Sergeant Major (E-9). I thought that it was a little odd that a Sergeant Major would be a First Sergeant (E-8) at the NSE.

On April 5ᵗʰ 2001, I left Pristina, Kosovo for the last time. That morning I ate breakfast at the dinning facility. I went to my old room, Paris 108, and packed my last items in my duffle. I locked the door and walked across the road to the bus stop. I placed my duffle near the stop sign. I saw a German solider waiting for the bus. I asked him to watch my duffle while I go to the housing office to turn in my room key and linen.

After I turned in the items, a Danish supply solider gave me a KFOR coin as a memento. I thanked him and went back to the bus stop. A few minutes passed by. I looked around Film City and saw soldiers and the many buildings that sprang up during the past year. I watched helicopters in the air. I listened to the noisy generators. All of this was a part of my life for a year in Kosovo.

The van pulled up. In the van's window a sign read 'Skopje'. The driver parked the van and got out to stretch in what was going to be my last two-hour bus ride. I put my bags in the back of the van. As I closed the door, there was CPT Jung standing at the bus stop with tears in her eyes. This was another 'Hollywood moment'. She was due to leave the following week. We hugged and I told her goodbye. It would be the last time I saw her.

The driver started the van. I got on the van along with two Germans, a British, Turkish and Spanish soldier. The van turned the corner and headed out the gate. In the distance, I saw two boys frantically waving at the van to stop.

The driver stopped. I saw Fisnic and Valon (Chapter 9) running towards the van. I got out and gave them a big hug. They gave me a present. It was a clock that had a map of Kosovo inside it with their signatures on the back. They wished me the best. I thanked them and returned to the van.

Life in Film City continued as normal, just like it always will. For a few minutes, time stood still for me. As the dust flew from our tires, I could not help but to think about the first time I arrived. So much has changed and so many things have grown. I too had change, maybe forever.

I had said goodbye to so many people it was tough on me. It was extremely tough because I knew that unlike my other past jobs I had in the states where I could visit anytime; I would never go back to Kosovo.

Kosovo will always be a part of me.

I flashed the 'peace' sign to Valon as we headed to Skopje.

26

"You sign here"

There is no rest for the weary. I had been on the go for the past two and a half years. With schools, training exercises and the long deployment, I really needed a rest but there were so many things that had to be done. I am facing a movement across the seas alone for the first time in my career. I am going on a cruise. I also wanted to make sure that my soon to be ex wife did not change her mind about me getting custody of the Bo.

I returned to Stuttgart to my virtual empty home. As soon as I unpacked from Kosovo, I traveled to the legal office on the army barracks to ask questions. I had in my hand the separation papers. They were drawn up while I was in Kosovo. Now, I wanted to get a divorce as quickly as possible.

The legal office told me that I needed to bring my soon to be ex wife with me on my next visit. I was informed that they had to notarize our separation agreement and needed both of our signatures. They also informed me that if we wanted a divorce, and my soon to be ex wife was staying in Germany; I had to file an uncontested divorce in the states.

I made an appointment at the legal office to get the separation papers signed.

That weekend, I went to her house to pick up the Bo. I told her that I made an appointment to see the legal office on Wednesday at 11:00 a.m. I asked her if she still had a copy of the separation agreement I mailed to her while I was in Kosovo. She said that she looked at it, but wanted to take another look at the forms.

It was at this point of our conversation that I did not want to make her upset about my plans on getting custody of the Bo. So when the subject came up I walked on eggshells, trying not to stir up any bad feelings.

I told her to look over the documents again and if she had any questions she could call me. She looked at her calendar. "Wednesday will be fine. I will catch the bus and meet you there," she said.

'Potential Problems'

Every weekend that I traveled to her house I was facing a potential two-part problem.

The first problem I had was picking the Bo up from his mother's apartment. When I knocked on her door, I could tell if her boyfriend was there. If he was there, then she would crack open the door, peering out of it. Then she would quickly close the door and inform the Bo I was at the door. He would have his overnight bag with him, as he would bust through the door with excitement. I don't know what I would had done if I would seen her boyfriend sitting in her apartment on a top of my furniture, I might had whipped his ass.

When her boyfriend was not there she would allow me to come in. As I walked in the door and through the living room to the Bo's room, I would notice all of our old things that we had shared for years. This would take a lot out of me seeing these items.

There was six crystal glasses that we got when we went to Prague.

A tea set that I got in the states.

A hand made rug that I got from Germany. "Wait a minute! Didn't I buy rug for myself? Damn, I think I did. It doesn't matter," I told myself.

The second problem was that the Bo had been with his mother for a long time and they had a routine. I wanted to know what they did so I could keep constant the things he was used to. The one thing we kept constant was the 'bedtime routine'.

That routine consisted of reading. I would read to him one night and he would read to me the next night. After the story, we talked about anything he wanted to talk about. Most nights I talked about going to the states. I told him that I would try and make life better for him. I told him not to be afraid.

In reality, I was afraid; I didn't know how to cook. I had to learn and practice patience. I had to remember to count to ten before I would lose my temper.

Tuesday was a long night for me. Thoughts ran through my mind all night. Was I such a bad guy? Did I treat her so badly? At what point did she fall out of love with me? When did she fall in love with this guy? Will I find happiness? Will I learn to be a Mr. Mom? Would the Bo get along with his new friends? Will he want to stay in the US? Will he want to go back to his mom? Will I make it?

Wednesday came. My face had lines in it from my sleepless night. I washed up and put my clothes on. I left early so I won't be late for our appointment at the legal office. Once I got to the office it was 10:15 a.m. I looked in the office and I did not see her. I took a seat outside the office and glanced at a newspaper. For some reason I could not concentrate. I felt nervous. Now I had thoughts of her not showing up. I started to panic.

The time was 10:19 a.m. I stood up and paced a bit. I tried not to look at my watch. After what seem like hours, I took a look at the clock that was hanging on the wall. The time was now 10:23 a.m. every minute felt like an hour. I decided to go for a walk. It would get my mind off of things.

I walked to the Post Exchange, which was about two blocks from the legal office. It had been over a year since I had been there. I walked in to the electronics department. (For some reason, I always end up there.) I looked at the new TVs and the new CDs. I could tell that I had been away for a while because everything looked so 'new' to me. I walked around like a kid in a candy store. New sales were on the latest computers. There were new speakers, new receivers and new DVD players.

Then I looked at my watch. I was 10:55 a.m.! I had just enough time to run back to the legal office. I shot out of the exchange door. I ran the two blocks back down the road. I arrived right at 11:00 a.m. Out of breath; I climbed the stairs to find her looking at me. "Where have you been? You can't even get here in time for something as important as this," she said. "Just like old times," I said quietly to myself, "she is pissed at me until the end."

I asked her if she looked at the separation agreement. She pulled it out of a folder. She took a minute and before she could answer, I heard someone yelled, 'Artis.'

It was the legal assistant. She motioned for us to come up to the desk. I was a little embarrassed. As we walked up to the desk, I saw other people looking at us. I did not know why there were there, but I felt like everyone knew why we were there.

"Ok, you are filing a separation agreement," as the clerk voice boomed throughout the room. I tried to speak softly as to keep the other people out of my business. "Yes." I whispered. "Did both of you read and agree to the agreement?" Again the clerk's voice roared like we were in a rock concert. "Yes." I said, in a barley auditable voice. "Ma'am, have you read and agreed to the agreement?" the clerk asked.

She paused and looked at the paperwork. I saw a moment of confusion then a look of sorrow. I said to myself 'don't tell me she had changed her mind?'

Finally, in what seemed like ten minutes she said 'yes'. "Ok, I need you to initial every page and you sign here; on the back page," the clerk said. She handed her a pen. My soon to be ex wife initialed every page and signed the back page. Then it was my turn. Afterwards the clerk went to the back and had it notarize.

The clerk handed each one of us a copy and said, "When you get to your next assignment in the states, you will file this at the county clerks' office. Each state is different in which you will have to wait until you will be granted a divorce. The clerks office will have all the information for you."

I thanked the clerk for broadcasting our business to the entire Stuttgart area and we left. As we turned around to walk out, everyone looked at us. I never felt so embarrassed in my life.

27

Leaving Germany

I needed and wanted to fill an empty house with furniture. My walls looked so empty with out my Shurank (wall unit) and I wanted to buy a new one along with a curio cabinet. I chose to buy these items from the same place where I bought my grandfather clock. This place was called Dold Exquisite. They make great German furniture that comes *'direct from the black forest'*. I wanted to have that certain look of uniformity.

However, I could not decide on a living room set. The PX furniture did not fancy me, so I decided to wait until I got to the states. In the meantime, I was also looking at beds for the Bo and myself. I didn't like the ones at the PX, or the ones I saw advertised in the newspaper. I went to a couple of German stores. How quickly I forgot that the majority of those beds are low and the sizes are very narrow.

I really wanted to buy new and long lasting items. I always told myself after my soon to be ex wife took most of the things in the house that this furniture is the 'this is it' furniture. I will not buy anything just to get me by. This furniture would (I hope) last a long time.

On my many journeys of shopping, I began to buy things for the 'house'. I bought Lladro figures. These will go with the ones that I already have. One day I bought almost 1,000 dollars worth figurines.

I went to the Stuttgart bazaar on the army post. Mr Abdulla was selling rugs and I feel in love with them. I bought a huge hand made Oriental rug that day. It started as one rug, then another. The next thing I knew, the Bo and I were traveling to other cities to find these rugs. On certain weekends we would make the trip to Heidelberg to meet with him. I ended up with seven of these beautiful Chinese rugs.

Break out the day planner

I ordered my curio cabinet and my wall unit. It would be delivered on April 26. When it came, I filled it with my 18 pieces of Lladro and items from I bought from Greece, Germany, Kosovo, Macedonia and the States.

I was due to leave Germany in mid June. I needed to sit down and plan on when I should pack up and ship my items to Fort Lewis, Washington. I went to the transportation office and found out that it would take about 75 days for household items to arrive. It would take about 60 days for my car to get there. It seemed like I have one hundred appointments. So, I got a planner. With thoughts gathered, my planner looked something like this:

For the month of April:

17th: pay off shurank and curio cabinet.
19th: Appointment (info) on shipping Household goods and car 8:30 a.m.
20th: Customs briefing 9:00 a.m. Parent/teacher conference at the Bo's school at 10:30 a.m.
24th: Awards Ceremony at 3:30 p.m. The Bo's school art gallery exhibit at 6:30 p.m.

For the month of May:

1st: Turn in army equipment.
2nd: 'Kids in the gym' at Bo's school at 2:0 p.m.
3rd: Go to military housing to get info on military furniture delivery.
8th: Get a/c in car fixed at 7:00 a.m. 10:00 a.m. meeting with Non-Commissioned Officers.
14th: Pay for trip to Jamaica!!!!! Turn in more equipment at 9:00 a.m.
15th: 7:00 a.m. meeting. 11:00 a.m. pre inspection of Class A uniform.
17th: 6:30 a.m. Class A inspection. Teach class on 'Kosovo duties of soldiers' 9:00 a.m.
18th: Pick up 'clearing papers'. These papers give you a list of whom you need to see before you leave. They also require signatures from many offices throughout Stuttgart.
22-23rd: Household items are packed up! Military furniture delivery on 23rd
24th: Clean up house, throw remaining items away/sell them/giveaway.
25th: Same as above. Go to travel office. Give flight info to agent.
29th: Make appointment of 'clearing' government quarters 10:00 a.m.
31st: Safety day at 9:00 a.m.

For the month June:

1st: Pay in advance for hotel room. $49.00 per night.
4th: Call Fort Lewis Lodge for reservations.
5th: Clear Post Exchange; pick up army records.
6th: Turn in car for shipping to the states at 9:00 a.m. Catch the bus back to my apartment. Pre inspection check (housing) at 1:00 p.m. Pick up Sergeant Dothard's car. (She was so nice in letting me borrow her car for a week!)
7th: Pick up airline tickets; Pick up dental records.
8th: Farewell dinner for co-worker at 6:30 p.m.
12th: 'Clear Quarters' at 1:00 p.m.; move into hotel room.
14th: Pick up medical records; get the Bo's school records and his shot record. At 2:30 p.m. 'Final out' processing. At this point and time I should have all required signatures on my clearing papers. Pick up the Bo from soon to be ex wife's place. Final goodbye!
15th: Fly to the states, leave Stuttgart 11:35 a.m.; arrival in Frankfurt 12:30 a.m.; leave Frankfurt 1:15 p.m. arrive in the states 3:45 p.m. Eastern Standard Time!!!

Somehow, I made all of this happen!

28

More Plans

While in Kosovo, I guess you could tell that I was very bitter in the way my soon to be ex wife and I broke apart. I admit it, when I got my head together I wanted to make her feel as bad as I did. I wanted her to say to me that she made the biggest mistake in doing what she had done. I wanted her to realize that life after her was not going to stop for me; only better. I wanted to elevate beyond my (and her) expectations.

My plans were coming together at break neck speed. I gave you a glance at my day planner for a few months. Let me give you a few more weeks:

July

15th: Arrive in DC; 'Levern' will pick up the Bo and me.
15th–24th Visit White House, Smithsonian Museums, Zoo, Space Center, take in an IMAX movie, Lincoln and Jefferson Museums, go to Capital Hill.
24th drive 'Levern's car to moms house; visit my daughter.
25th Go to my favorite mall (Mac Arthur mall in Norfolk) and look at bedroom furniture.
27th Pick up 'Levern' from bus station.
28th–July 1st Jamaica!

July

2nd Take 'Levern' and the Bo to my first radio station (WFOS) Take them to where I grew up on Main Creek road. Stop by Norfolk State University and check out radio station WNSB. Take them to my last job before I joined the army, WTVZ-Ch 33.

3rd Drive to Lexington, Virginia and stay at the Hampton Inn for the 4th. Visit Virginia Military Institute. Show 'Levern' the house that I had lived in. See if the Bo can remember any of it.

4th Drive to Bowie, Maryland.

Before I left Germany (July 14) the last thing I gave my wife was this schedule. When she looked at it, her mouth dropped open. Her only come back was "this should be great for the Bo." Then she said, "Oh, you are going to Jamaica?" as if it was not true.

Even if she did not believe it, it felt good to see her reaction on her face. Mission one complete. I was in pay back mode.

My next part of the plan was to purchase bedroom furniture. I found a site on the Internet. This place was called Restoration Furniture. They had a location in Norfolk. I picked out the items that I really like. I ended up buying a King size bed along with a 6 drawer chest.

Jamaica and the summer

My mother kept the Bo for four days while 'Levern' and I went on our trip to Jamaica. We had a great time in Jamaica. I snorkeled for the first time in my life; I think I drank half of the Atlantic Ocean. We went on trips and we climbed the Ochos Rios falls. We spent nights in a hammock. We ate awesome food (jerk chicken was the best).

There was a Tai restaurant that was about 800 yards from our resort. The restaurant was in a shallow part of the ocean. Still it was deep enough that the only way you could get to it was by boat. We had a great evening there. It was in this place that I knew 'Levern' was the woman for me. I could talk about anything and she made me feel at ease around her.

One evening the resort closed its three main restaurants and prepared a spread of food that I have never seen before. There were many different foods. A children's band played for us. The evening was capped off with a dance and a fire-eater!

The back door to our room was about ten feet from the beautiful blue water. I have never seen water that blue. The water was warm and it felt great to be in it.

We ate breakfast on the patio. We danced. We played games with the other couples that were there. We even participated in a 'swap clothes' event on the beach. All in all, the four days and three nights were too short, but at least we experienced the warm feelings that Jamaica gave us and we did not want to leave. It was so good to experience this with someone that you care about.

When we came back to the states, there was no rest for the weary. We traveled to the place where I grew up. My neighborhood, Crest Harbor, is where I have written many stories about my Mom and Dad. I showed 'Lerven' my folk's house that we use to live in for over twenty years. She met some of my friends. We spent the rest of the day traveling to the TV and radio stations that I use to work for.

We made the trip to VMI in Lexington, VA. If you ever get a chance to travel, do yourself a favor and get up there. It is very beautiful and it is full of history. It has an old town feel to it. Stores are neatly fitted on a few streets and it is within walking distance to some of the great restaurants. 'Levern' fell in love with the town.

I parked my car across the street from my old house on Nelson Street. Not much has changed. The Bo remembered our big back yard. Off to the side of the yard was a huge depression. Back when I was living there, I used to call that depression the 'bowl'.

For a mid day snack, we walked to the ice cream parlor and had scoops of ice cream. In the background was Washington and Lee University. Once we got back to the car, we drove to VMI where they had hot air balloons on the grounds along with an old time picnic for the 4th of July. I saw many friends there. The next day, we drove back to 'Levern's house in Maryland. The Bo and I spent another ten days before we were off to Fort Lewis, Washington.

The last part of the plan, was once I arrived at Fort Lewis, get a divorce.

29

The fear of being a single dad

The summer vacation went all to fast; now my greatest fear that was facing me was becoming a single dad. I wish I could have read a book on it because I knew nothing about this topic. For me this is definitely uncharted water. I thought about my father and I knew that I did not want to raise my son like he did me.

Now it was my turn not only to be a man, but also a single parent. I was afraid. I must give a lot of credit to my soon to be ex wife. From the very beginning she suggested that we talked to the Bo. We did not use a lot of 'kiddy' words when he was younger. We did not sugar coat much. That help me a great deal because now I needed him to understand what we are facing, together.

Before our flight, I found a quiet room and I sat him down and talked to him. This was my first father and son talk. I guess this was the first thing in becoming a single dad; an open line of communications. I told him that I would try not to let him down. I told him that I would never hurt him. Most of all, I told him that I loved him so much that we will make it through this. If he ever got lonely he could call his mom and talk to her. I would never stand in his way if he wanted to talk to her.

I wanted to talk to her as well for any 'pointers' I could use. I made a promise to myself that I will never 'bad mouth' my soon to be ex wife when the Bo was in my company.

Onward to Lewis

I called ahead and spoke to MSG Pelt. He would pick the Bo and I from the airport and serve as a military 'sponsor' for my new unit. A sponsor is the person that welcomes us to a new assignment like Ft. Lewis but also answers questions about the unit and the area. He is the 'go to' person whenever you need help. He will be part tour guide and part answer man.

We thanked 'Levern' for a great time as we departed BWI airport for SeaTac airport. Our flight was on time, but we had a long lay over in Atlanta. We had some hot dogs and we walked around the airport. A couple of hours later our flight was due to leave. I was reading a magazine at one of the newspaper kiosks, when the Bo asked for some candy, which I bought him. We got on the plane and headed for SeaTac.

Mid flight the stewardess brought us our dinner. He and I ate. A few minutes later the Bo said he was about to throw up. The first thing that I told him was to 'Hold it'. As soon as I told him that, he let it fly. I was embarrassed. I apologized to the man that sat next to us. I told myself, '**Lesson one** as a single parent; don't over feed the Bo on long trips'.

I washed him up in the small latrine. Still he smelled a bit. I reminded MSG Pelt about our airplane incident when we landed at SeaTac. It was well past 1:00 a.m. when we got to our hotel room at Ft. Lewis. We were beat. My first day as single dad was complete.

Morning came too quick. The Bo was sleeping so peaceful. I looked at him for about five minutes. It was the first time that I watched him sleep like that since he was a baby. "Well this is it. He and I are all alone and I will have to do a lot of things by myself. I think I can do it," I whispered to myself. I washed up while he was still sleeping. I heard my stomach growl. I looked in the small fridge. It was empty. I thought first things first. I need to find somewhere to get breakfast.

I stepped out of the bathroom. The Bo was half sleep. "Are you hungry Bo?" I asked. A weak 'yes' came across his mouth. I called room service to find out about breakfast. The lady told me that they did not serve any meals and Burger King and the commissary was down the street. I told him to wash up and we would go to BK. He jumped out of bed and was ready to go within minutes.

Lesson two; I can get the Bo to dress faster if I mention any kind of fast food. I knew that I had to curb the convenience of any fast food and learn how to cook.

After breakfast, I stopped at the front desk to pick up a local map. The lady at the desk told me that according to army policy, I had to be out of the lodge by 6th of August. That was within ten days.

I shifted my focus of getting my son and I a temporary house or apartment to stay. I knew that I eventually wanted to live on post. I also knew that there was going to be a 'waiting list' of available houses that were on post. I went back to my room and called MSG Pelt. He told me that he would stop by within the hour to get me started 'in processing' into Ft. Lewis.

There was no place where I could drop the Bo off, so I had to drag him everywhere I went that day. The first place we went to was the welcome center. The welcome center was across the street from the lodge. When I walked into the center, I received a list of items that I had to complete within a week.

We went to the finance office. That took about an hour. MSG Pelt stayed and answered my questions about Ft. Lewis and the surrounding area. He was very helpful to me. He told me that he would check on us later.

The next stop was the medical station. The line was so long and the Bo was getting fussy. I told him that if he had to be a 'big boy' and be patience. We waited for almost an hour and a half when were finally seen.

It was getting close to lunchtime. I had a feeling with all the information I had to get like housing, schools, daycare, picking up my car from the port, getting equipment, checking to see if my household items made it and going to many briefs, I needed a child care provider.

I asked around and I found the office where I could get some help. I explained that I was a single parent and I needed some one to watch the Bo during the day. I enrolled him into a daycare He would start the next day.

During lunch, I bought some items from the commissary and started the afternoon with more in processing. I stopped by the housing office and put my name on the waiting list. My number was 98. That meant 97 people ahead of me were waiting for housing as well. I picked up a 'renters sheet' of houses and apartments. This was a list of reputable renters that were in the area. I called and made appointments to look at these places later in the week.

My car made in from Germany and I arranged to pick it up the next day. Once I got back to the hotel, I called the first name I saw on the 'renters sheet'. I spoke to a nice lady that was renting a house in Lakewood, Washington. Lakewood was only a ten-minute drive from Ft. Lewis.

She told me that I could come over within an hour. I wrote down the address. I left early, as I wanted to see the outside of the house and get a look at the neighborhood.

The neighborhood was rather quiet. I stood outside of the home for about ten minutes. The lady drove up, and I introduced myself. We walked towards the house. The house was rather old but it was just fine for the Bo and me. Inside, the rooms were small but had a big back yard complete with a basketball hoop and an apple tree.

I explained to her that I was in need of something quick and was not going to be renting for long because I put my name on the housing list. She had people like me who rented from her and she understood my problem. We agreed to a monthly lease and quickly made the deal.

She asked me when I could move in. I told her that I needed to check to see if my household items were in and would call her tomorrow. I gave her a deposit for a three-bedroom 800 square foot house.

Running from point A to point Z.
(Mo' money, mo' problems)

The next day was filled with more in processing. I went to the transportation office to see if my household items made it. "It has been in storage for about a week. When do you need the items delivered?" the clerk asked. I asked to use his office phone. I called the landlord but her phone was busy. I told him that I had to check back with him within a couple of hours.

I then realized that I needed a cell phone. Off I went to the PX and bought a fairly good phone. I made contact with the landlord and told her the news. We agreed that I could move in on August 6th. That is the last day I could be in the hotel. Things were going smoothly but a little hectic.

You would not believe what I had to go through to get the Bo enrolled in the school at Ft. Lewis! I am not going to go through the entire process. That would take a chapter alone.

In a nut shell there was a little confusion because I live off post and I was requesting that he go to Beachwood elementary school on post. I had to enroll him first at Clover Park elementary (in Lakewood) so (I guess) to get him in the school district/system. After I had the blessing from the administration office at Clover Park to 'let' him attend Beachwood it was settled. I turned the paper work in to Beachwood's admin office. I was told that he needed a physical. I made the appointment for the 8th of August. Then he would be 'good to go' to attend school.

Another problem I had was to get my car registered in Washington. I went to the motor vehicle office to purchase tags for my car. After standing in line for twenty minutes (I don't like lines, just like my grandmother and father!) I was turned around. I needed to go to the port where I picked up my car for more paperwork that I should had received the first time. This was frustrating. Every two steps I took, I was going back one. After I got the paperwork I had to pay big bucks for the tags.

The new cell phone was being used a lot. Since I did not have a home phone, my cell phone bill was going to be huge. I made an appointment to get a house phone turn on the 6th of August. I called the cable company. They could not connect the cable until the 15th of the month. No TV with an 8 year old for 10 days was going to be tough!

I notified the water and electric company that I was moving in August. I drove by and made a deposit to the companies.

I called Restoration Hardware for my delivery on my king sized bed. They were having problems with me buying the bed in Virginia where state tax was at 4%. In Washington, the state tax was 8%. They wanted the difference between the two. After many calls we came to an agreement. That delayed the arrival of my bed. It was pushed back two weeks. That meant the Bo and I would be sleeping my very old love seat and couch.

I had the bed scheduled, but it did not come with a mattress. I went to sleep mattress discounters. They made their mattresses on the premises. It took a week for the mattress to be made and I had it delivered the same day that the bed was to arrive at the house. The mattress alone cost just over 1,000 bucks!

After a week of in processing and living in a suitcase for ten days, it was time for us to move in our new temporary house. The movers called the Friday before we move out of the hotel and told me that they would be at the house around 9:00 a.m. August the 6th. It was all set.

We left the hotel at 7:00 a.m. and went to McDonalds for breakfast. Then we went to the new house. I let the Bo pick out his room. The movers came on time. They were really happy to find out that I did not want most of my items unpacked. I picked out the items that were needed the most. Since there was no bedroom furniture the move took half the day. The items I did not want unpack were put in the garage.

That night was my first night as dad and mom. I made the slow walk to the kitchen. The stove looked big. I looked in the fridge to find out what I was going to prepare for dinner. The Bo told me that he was hungry. My palms were sweaty. I forgot that the microwave I had in Germany did not work and I needed a new one. I told him that we had to go to the PX and buy one.

We bought the microwave. It was getting late. I told him that Burger King was cooking and we will go there to have 'dinner' there. I had avoided cooking dinner for one more night.

The next day was spent putting things in its place. The house was small but had a 'homey' feel to it. Before I left Germany, I made an agreement with my soon to be ex wife that she could have one of two American TVs and the VCR. The reason for this is when we got settled in our new place, I was going to send her a video of him. If you lived overseas you know VCR's systems are a little different. The US has the NTSC system. Germany has the PAL system. So if I was to make a video of him with her German system she could not see the videotape.

The reason why I brought this up is that we did not have cable and it was a little boring. I had the other TV and a small DVD player. When we unpacked his items, all of his movies were on videotape. Point being is we went back to the PX to buy the Bo a VCR/DVD player. He wanted to me to buy him a couple of DVD movies. Of course the ones he had at home weren't new enough! Man, this is really getting expensive!

That night I had to cook. No more excuses of running out for something we needed for the house and ending up at another fast food place. I told myself to fix a meat portion and a vegetable portion.

That night I cooked a 'steak um' with toast and corn. Breakfast was no problem. That is the one thing I can cook is bacon and eggs. Cereal was always big with him.

One night after dinner, the Bo was sleeping on the old love seat and I slept on the couch. I was so tired from all the in processing at Ft. Lewis. I was so overwhelmed from all of the household needs. I had to remember to get a newspaper subscription, call the garbage collectors to find out when they picked up the trash. I needed to find someone to cut the grass, or buy a lawn mower. The refrigerator was really empty. The cupboards were bare. The Bo needed new clothes to wear.

Then I heard a loud thump. He had rolled off the love seat. He kept sleeping without missing a beat. I put him back on the love seat.

The next day we I went out to buy an inflatable (small) mattress. That night he slept on it. The next morning he was under it.

Ten days later, we finally got the cable, the king size mattress and bed. It felt so good to watch news and some of his favorite programs. It felt better to get a good night sleep. Through it all we kept the same routine of reading before bed.

After reading and before he would go to sleep we would spend a few moments talking about what we did today and what we were going to do tomorrow. I would ask him what was the best thing he did today. Then I would ask him what he did not like. I asked him if he misses his mom. We would hug and I would kiss him on the cheek. We would tell each other goodnight.

Lesson three; keep old routines; they never die.

Our little temporary house was taken shape. I got better (yeah, right) as a cook. The Bo and I would play basketball in the backyard in the evenings. 'Levern' and I talked every night.

The Bo started school. **Lesson four;** when he had homework, I also had homework. When we got home, he would go in the back yard and play while I fixed dinner. After dinner, I washed the plates and he did his homework. Later, we would go over his homework. He would then take a bath and lay out his school clothes for the next day. He would usually be in bed by 8:45 p.m. just enough time for me to collapse on the couch and get myself ready for the next day.

Lesson five; always have the Bo to lie out his clothes the night before; if he gets up late at least we know what he is wearing.

On the weekends, we would go to Seattle. We went on a tour of Safeco field. (The Mariners baseball stadium) We went to Mount Rainer. We went to an IMAX movie. We went to the experience music project, (EMP) which is one of the coolest places I had ever been. We went on top of the space needle. We always had a great time.

One day I looked in the phone book under 'divorce'. I called several attorneys to get a set price. "Man, this is another expenditure that I really can't afford," I told myself. "I may need to go to the legal office on post."

The following Monday, I went to the legal office on post. I quickly found out that I could 'represent' and do it myself with help from the legal office at Ft. Lewis. I was informed that the clerk that types the divorce decree had a death in the family and I needed to wait a few weeks until she returned. Because of this, she was behind in her appointments. My appointment was in the middle of October.

The Bo and I were finally settling in our own place. Our routine was very easy and we spent a lot of time together. He was like my best friend. I told him a lot of things and had the chance to ask or answer questions. We grew very close and we were the perfect father and son team. He was very interested in basketball. I taught him how to shoot and play defense. The weather was very nice and we played a lot in the back yard.

It had been a little more than a month and I called the housing office to see where I was on the list. I had move up to number 93. I asked the clerk to give me a good guess when I would be living on post. He told me with in a month. I could not believe it! How could I jump ahead that many people that was before me. He told me that many people often change their minds about living on post. Some people bought houses, and others were locked in a yearly lease. Since I signed a monthly lease, I could be in on post housing quickly.

September 11th

'Levern' and I were making plans to see each other. I was all set up in the house so I invited her to come out and see us. She checked the airline prices. She also got time off from working at her job, which was located in downtown DC. Then something terrible happened.

I think every American will never forget where they were when we were hit by the terrorist's attacks. I was standing in our morning physical fitness formation. You have to keep in mind that I was in Washington State. It was about 6 a.m. when one of the soldiers told us about it. We all left to get dress in our uniforms. Since I lived off post and I had to get my military uniform, I made the 10-minute drive to my house.

When I got home I turned on the TV, I was shocked to see the images. I could not believe what was happening. I quickly got dressed and headed back to work. I had the radio blaring. I was hoping, praying that many lives were spared.

Then I heard that a plane had crashed into the Pentagon! My heart raced. Where are they going to attack next? What is going on? Once I got to I-5 and was heading towards Ft. Lewis, the traffic was at a stand still. I called my unit (which was a Military Police unit) to find out what was going on. I was told that the MP's was checking every car coming through the gate. My normal ten-minute ride to Ft. Lewis ended up being two hours!

Later on that day, I called 'Levern'. She worked about 6 blocks down from the White House. They had to evacuate the building she worked in. She told me of the chaos of people running in the streets. The Metro system was shut down, but she got a ride from a friend of hers. It was a freighting day for all of us.

When I picked up the Bo, his teacher told the students what had happen. He asked, "Papa, what is going on? Who are the people that are doing this to us?"

I told him that there are people that want to do us harm. I told him I did not know what is going on but he will be safe.

Not only do I have the fear of being a single dad but now I had the fear of the unknown.

30

Making moves

The Bo and I had made videotape for my soon to be ex wife but I did not sent it to her. I wanted to wait until we moved to our new house. I gave a quick glance around the old house just to give her a sample of how we were living in Lakewood, Washington.

'Levern' flew to Washington the day when the FAA allowed flying to resume after the terrorist attacks. She told me that the plane was less than half full and the service was excellent. I picked her up and drove her to Lakewood. I showed 'Levern' our small house.

The next day I received a call from the housing office at Ft. Lewis. The clerk told me that they had a place for me if I was interested in living on post! Excited, I told them yes!

"How soon could I move in?" I asked. The clerk told me within two weeks and he gave me the address of our new place. I told 'Levern' about it and within a flash we were off to Ft. Lewis to take a look at our new place. We got the keys and when we walked the new house I automatically started placing furniture. The new place was a much bigger three-bedroom house with over 1000 square feet.

I made a call to the housing office to arrange our move. The military would pay for our move on post and 'Levern' agreed to stay and extra week to help with the move.

I had more things to do before the move. I called the water and the electric company to inform them of the move. I called the phone company to get a new phone number. I called the cable company to switch service from one house to another. I had the newspaper to deliver the paper to our new address.

Because 'Levern' was at Ft. Lewis with me, things were much easier. During the evenings, we had long talks. It was nice to share things with her and now our relationship started to get more serious.

The Final Purchases

After the move on post and boxes were put up and paper was thrown away, I sat back and took a look around the house. There were items that I still needed to buy. I went to the furniture store to buy a new living room sofa and love seat. At another store I got the Bo a queen-sized bed.

The house at Ft. Lewis had poor overhead lighting so I needed lamps. In the past I had two Tiffany style lamps that I used in the bedroom on my small dresser and nightstand. So to stay consistent, I purchased five more Tiffany style lamps for the entire house. I even bought the Bo a Tiffany style night-light for his room. At night, these lamps looked so well when they were on that it always set a certain atmosphere. I also purchased candles from my favorite candle store 'Illuminations'. I am such a sucker for these candles. When I shopped there the ladies would have big bags ready for me.

The next and final purchase that I needed to make was for the walls. I had these old posters and pictures from many years; I decided to throw them out. I wanted to start new. I decided to buy art.

I had always admired Charles Bibbs. He quickly became my favorite artist. I purchased so many paintings by him; I am embarrassed to tell you how many I own. His art is so expressive and has many colors that complement my furniture.

I also purchased two items by my second favorite artist C' Babi Bayoc. I bought two buffalo soldier prints by Don Stivers and one by Justin Bua.

The house was set. 'Levern' left after two weeks but cooked enough food for us so I would not have to cook for a while. It was now back to being Mr. Mom again.

By the middle of October I received a call from the legal office. My divorce papers were ready for my review. I made the appointment and a few days later I walked in. A bit nervous, I read the seven separate documents that had to be filed in the county court clerks' office.

I signed the documents and made an additional two copies. The original had to be filed in court and the other two copies were for my soon to be ex wife and myself. I called her to explain what was coming by express mail and she had to sign the original copies and keep one for her records. I told her that I needed these back as soon as possible, so I can get on the court docket.

With a report card comes new rules

The Bo received his first report card in a new school system. It was not good. Well, it was not totally bad but it should have been better. I was upset. I called my mother and ask her what to do. She told me that everything was new and it would take time for him to adjust.

I laid down a few more rules. I was already reading to him at night and he read to me sometimes, but now things were going to be different. He started to read to me every night. If he had homework, he done it first before going out to play. Homework was done on the dining room (table) not in his room. During school nights, bedtime was changed from 9:30 p.m. to 9:00 p.m.

The final argument!!

I called my soon to be ex wife a few days later to see if she got the papers I sent earlier in the month. When she answered the phone I could hear the strain in her voice. She ripped into me right away.

"You are asking for child support and I don't have a job. You know I am not working right now so how do you expect me to send money to you," she yelled.

I could tell she was hotter than the sun right now. I needed her to calm down and get these papers signed. The longer it takes the longer we would have to wait for a divorce. Before I could get anything out she went into another tear.

"Why are you rushing me to get these papers signed? Do you want to get married? Have you found some one on post? Is she in the army? If not, she cannot live on post until you get married so why are you rushing me? I need time to look at everything. I can't rush into anything!" she said.

The first thought that jumped out at me was her comment on 'she can't rush into anything'. Wait a minute! Didn't she leave me for another man and had his baby and she doesn't want to be rushed? I tried to hold my cool but I was about to explode!

Then she jumped in again, "Do I have to sign all of these papers? Did the legal office help you? What does this mean? What does that mean? Blah, Blah, Blah...."

I was trying to count ten. I tried counting sheep. I held my breath but to no avail none of this worked.

I told her that I did not want any money from her, just the divorce. Hell, she is living with that guy, why can't I get on with my life?

She said, "You could change my mind and demand support."

She was right. I could change my mind, but money was not the issue. I did not expect any money from her anyway; I just wanted to be finally free of her.

She continued on and on about this and that, so I lost it.

Now we were in a heated battle. (Man this felt like old times!)

Right then, all of a sudden, she broke in to tell me that she wanted me to take a DNA test.

"For what?" I screamed.

"To prove that you are not the father of the baby that is here," she said.

"I am not spending a dime on any DNA test to prove I am not the father of that child. We only had unprotected sex **ONCE** and that was back in 1994. You know that, why are you asking me this?" I said.

She explained that there was a German law that I have to provide proof that I am not the father of her child. Since we are getting a divorce, she told me that if I do not have a DNA test, the baby would have **MY** last name!

I still refused. To this day I don't remember what I said exactly, but I let it fly. I said my peace then I hung up on her.

That was a mistake and I admit it, but for years we were both frustrated. She gave up on me a while back and now I wanted to get on with my life. She left me for someone, why can't I have someone and go it about it *legally*?

I had reached the end of my rope. I called her back to apologize. We talked peacefully and she told me that she would sign the papers and get them in the mail the next day. I told her that I would ask how much the DNA test would cost. I thought that I could get a test on post and it may be free.

I called the post hospital and found out that they don't test anyone for DNA unless in an extreme case. They referred me to the area DNA testing lab. I called the 800 number and found out that it would cost 1,000 bucks!

As I said before, I did not spend one dime and did not test!

I received the papers ten days later. I checked the entire documents to make sure that they were all signed. Every thing was just about set.

The following week I went to the circuit court. I filed on November 27th. Believe it or not that was a day after her birthday! I was informed that I had to wait 90 days (cooling off period) before the divorce would be final. I had to come back to court within two weeks of the final date to settle final payments and court cost.

It was now mid January. I stopped by the circuit court. I told the clerk that the divorce was going to be final. She asked me if I had any children. I told her yes. Then she threw me a curve ball.

She asked if I had attended the mandatory class that divorced parents had to go to. I said no and told her it was the first that I had heard about it. She told me that I needed this class before the judge would grant the divorce. The class would give me a certificate of proof that I was there. The class was four hours long and was held on different days and times. She gave me a schedule with all the information I needed. She told me that I needed to call right away because these classes filled up quickly (imagine that).

With my trusty cell phone I called around to see if I could get into any classes. The first three was booked solid! I called the Family Support Center located in Olympia, Washington. Luckily, I got the last slot. I asked one of my best friends if she could watch the Bo while I was going to the class. She told me yes.

I dropped off the Bo at my friends' house and went to the class. I sat in the front of the class, as everyone wanted to sit near the back. There were two instructors there. They introduced themselves. We watched a 20/20 ABC interview with kids that were going through divorce. Then we went into the basis of the class, 'Helping Children Through Divorce'.

To take a quote from the class "…you will be given information to assist your child thought the divorce process. Unfortunately, in addition to your world coming apart, your child's world is now breaking with your divorce. You cannot resolve their fears with a trip to Disney World, or buffer the blow at McDonald's. Their world is separated. It is the responsibility of both parents to learn cooperation and compromising skills. We commend you on taking this step to enhance your skills and learn new ways to support your child."

Damn, there is another mention of fast food in my world.

After the class I learned new ways to support the Bo. The class went into grief and loss, verbal and non-verbal communications, actively listening, problem solving, stress and most importantly blending families.

I was very happy that the state of Washington made me attend this class. I kept the book and referred to it often. With certificate in hand I am now ready and confident to take the next step in my life.

31

Divorce...damn, part two

It was a cold, windy but sunny day in February. Clothes packed nicely, neatly in the closet, but having a hard time deciding what to wear. Standing there with a blank stare into the abyss darkness of the closet, he finds a dark pair of pants with a matching shirt. Slowly but steadily he dresses himself as if this was his last meal, his last day on the earth. The heartbeat in his chest is pumping through his throat. He had thoughts swimming through his mind of twelve years of marriage ending on today. The day, this day would be his last day of 'married' life.

Out the house he walked, bumping in the door as he tried to close the door with him in it. It is as if he was sleep walking, having a very bad dream that he can't wake from. He starts the car. He sits in it for a while, staring blankly into the dashboard. He turns on the heat to warm himself. He steps on the gas while the car is in park. Heat slowly comes into the car. He backs the car out of the driveway and is on the way towards his destination.

It seems the car is driving its self as he weaves in and out of traffic. The radio is nonsexist at this point. He makes it to Tacoma's courthouse within twenty minutes finding a lucky free parking spot almost in front of the building. He walks out of the car into the building looking at the people looking at him. It is as if he was in a trance.

He checks the information board. He finds the judge's name with the courtroom he must appear. He checks his watch but can't figure out the time. The lights are bright, but his mind is dull. He looks at the clock on the wall. He figures out that he is early so he takes a seat across the courtroom.

He notices people walking into the courtroom as if they were in a trance as well. Men and women walking together but no words were spoken. The silence was deafening he wanted to yell out aloud 'someone say something!' He didn't. He noticed faces that was wrecked and strained with the pain that they were suffering. In one corner there was one lady that wept softly wiping her tears with a tissue. He wanted to stare but thought that it would be rude.

We filed into the room. On the board there were names. He saw 'Artis vs Artis' third to the bottom. It was going to be a long day. A few minutes later we heard 'all raise Judge S is presiding'. In unison we stood and sat down.

He is wondering what happened to these people's life. What did it take for them to be here today? Was it another person in their lives? Did they not get along? Did they get married for the wrong reason? At what point did they not try anymore.

The first case was that woman he noticed was crying earlier. She cried through the entire proceeding. When the judge asked if the marriage was forever broken she looked at her soon to be ex husband as to say 'lets give this on more try'. The man said yes it is forever broken. Then she gave a weak 'yes' in agreement. The Judge told them that they were divorced.

All of a sudden, his thoughts went back to 1986, his first day of basic training. The drill sergeant was yelling, cursing like crazy. The sergeant told everyone to get off the bus. That bus was known as the 'cattle car'. That name was meant for the poor privates that were going to be led to a 'slaughter' of a time at basic training. Some how he felt like this divorce was herding season for all that was in the courtroom. We'd 'buffaloed' in, to get a divorce, the judge grants it, and then we are 'buffaloed' out. Only to be followed by more people, many more people.

Another couple was led to the judge. The man who was getting a divorce looked happy. So did the woman. Their case went quickly. The Judge noticed that they had smiles on their faces, but the Judge was not pleased. He told them that they were divorced. His anger made him slammed his gavel down.

The noise broke my dream. Reality set in for me. For a second I thought that I was in my bed, but I was in the courtroom. I rubbed my eyes. Then I stood to look at the board that I thought I saw in my dream. I found my name and soon it would be my turn.

An hour later I heard the clerk loudly say, "The next case is Artis vs Artis." He pointed where I should stand. I looked at the Judge. I felt so tiny in his presence. I did not want to stare in his face, but I did anyway. I saw his big black robe. He looked up and asked me where was Mrs. Artis. I told him that she was still in Germany as he looked over the seven documents that I had filed earlier.

"I see that she is a German citizen, is that correct?" Judge S asked. "Yes sir." I said, "She decided that she wanted to live in Germany."

"Well, Mr. Artis, you will have to file another document stating that she is not here. You will have to get a notary public to witness it. At this time, take one of the forms that the clerk will give you, fill it out and go to room 130 to get it sworn into court. I will go to the next case and you will be the last case I will see today. Do you understand?" the Judge asked.

"Yes sir." I answered. I got the form and filled it out in the room and had it sworn into the court. I rushed back into the courtroom ten minutes later. There was another person that was also in the same position as me and the judge also sent him to room 130 to get his paperwork straighten out.

As soon as I sat down, Judge S called me to appear in front of him. As the Judge reviewed the paperwork he asked me did I attend the mandatory class for divorcing children. I told him yes and handed the clerk my certificate.

He quickly reviewed it and told me that all documents were in order. Then he asked me if the marriage was forever broken. I answered 'yes'. He told me that I was now divorced and wished me a good day.

That was it.

Five good minutes with the Judge and we were free.

I drove back to my place. I looked at the time. It was going on 5:00 p.m. on the west coast but it was 2:00 a.m. in Germany. I called 'Levern' and gave her the news. She asked me how I felt.

I replied, "Kind of weird, but we have been apart so long that it wasn't any big difference. Only now it is official." Then I called my mom and gave her the news. The next day I called my ex wife and gave her the news. I told her that I would mail her the official documents soon. Overall, we both took it like it was just another day.

Sizing things up

Back in the old days I use to walk the mall, cruise the beach or check out what was happening on campus at Norfolk State University. Back then; I was looking for a certain type of woman. I use to size a girl up first by the height and weight. Then I looked at color of skin and the beauty of her face. Ok, sometimes it would not be in that order.

If she was cute I tried to be all over her. I used those old school lines like, 'hey baby, what is your sign?' It never worked.

During my 'radio days' women would be interested in me because I could take them to concerts or give them free records. It was never about *me.* It was all about the free things I could get. There was no real love in any woman I met during those times.

Before I joined the army, women use to size me up. If I went to a club and I like what a woman was wearing or how she danced, or how she looked, I asked her if she would like to dance with me. Nine times out of ten I would be turned down. Then another guy would ask her the same question and she would dance with him. Now what in the hell was wrong with me? Was it because I was a short, dark skinned guy that did not act 'cool'? What the hell was 'cool' anyway?

When I joined the army, women use to size me up in another way. Take the same situation that I had mentioned before. While talking to any women, they would ask what type of car that I drove. They would ask how much money I was making and what my rank was. Hell, that offended me. What am I asking for a dance with a girl or am I applying for a job?

My forty acres and a mule

In my life there have been about three women that like me for me. No absurd questions. They just love me for what I was. It did not matter what type of car I drove or how much money I had in my pocket. It was a genuine love. 'Levern' is one of the three women I am speaking about. The other two were about twenty years ago.

'Levern' has shown me so much more love in the six months we'd been together than in the 12 years I was married to my ex wife. I hate to use that as a comparison, but it is true. This is so unusual seeing how much she loves me that I don't know how to react to it.

Most of my life has been a constant argument with either my parents and or my ex that it feels strange to be in this place of love and warmth. I did not ask 'Levern' for any of this. She has been married before. She informed me that her first marriage ended when her husband decided not to be a husband. As a devoted single working mother with one child she had very little time to develop meaningful relationships.

She was deployed to Macedonia as a reservist. After she got back from the Balkans, she returned to her old job, making pretty good money. She has many close and dear friends. Some of them she has known for over thirty years. Her daughter and her grandson lived very close to her and they visit often. She is willing to leave all of this to be with a short out of shape guy like me. Damn, that is love.

When you're not looking for love and suddenly find that you have it, these feelings feel so real.

So I sized up the situation and asked myself, does this seem so fast, so all of a sudden? Do I need a timetable? I just officially got out of a marriage. Do I need a break?

I asked my mom the same question. She told me that I might never, ever have a chance or an opportunity like this to be happy. I agreed. I better reel 'Levern' in before someone else who may not be looking for anyone, takes her away from me.

I proposed. I popped the question. She said yes! I told her just to bring herself and her clothes. The house was all ready and set for her.

The Bo's schoolwork began to improve. He was doing well in school and was very happy. I told him that he would have a new stepmother. He didn't even break stride in his response. He ask me who is it? I told him 'Levern' and he said, 'ok'.

Soon, the Bo, 'Levern' and I were to be a family. 'Levern' had the most work on her end. She had to sell her apartment, sell most things in her house and give notice at her job. On our end, there wasn't much to do. I had to make room for her with closet space and other odds and ends.

Two months later 'Levern' arrived for good. 'Levern' and I set an April wedding date. Everything was going well. 'Levern' gave our house that 'woman' feel too it. She added more things to my sparse kitchen. She was a cleaning and cooking freak. I like that. Most importantly, the Bo and she got along great.

In April we married. Her best friend of 30-years, Sha Ron, was the maid of honor. Sergeant First Class Kenneth Jackson was my best man and Sergeant Christopher 'Mother' Hubbard along with his fiancée were the witnesses.

The ceremony was short and sweet. It was wonderful. This time I was confident that 'Levern' and I really understood our vows (you may find that reference in a past chapter in this book).

After the wedding we headed to a fantastic restaurant located just south of Seattle. The name of the place was called 'Salty's on Akli Beach. Man that was some good food.

Now, I have everything, a good son, a loving wife, a happy household, and my forty acres and a mule. Is this a dream? Everything is going so perfectly!

Or is it?

32

The season of discontent

As the old saying goes, the best way to a man's heart is through his stomach. 'Lev-ern' not only can cook but she keeps a clean house. Before she arrived, there wasn't much to my cooking, so there wasn't much to clean especially in the kitchen.

This was too easy. I could not believe how everything fell into place so quickly. 'Levern', the Bo and I were learning each other and spending a lot of time together.

The Bo had a lot of friends and they were coming to the house often. He really got into playing basketball. I took him to the gym at least twice a week and he would shoot baskets. The neighbor across the street bought one of those portable basketball hoops. The Bo and his friends would stay out there all night and shoot hoops if I would let him.

Tired from a half-day of school and doing homework and playing basketball into the late evening would drain him. I guess he did not have time to miss his mom. Still, we were living in the Pacific Northwest where we are happy to see the sun a few days out of the month.

When it rained and he could not go outside, it was tough on him. I think during these times he missed her most. He would come in our room and tell me that he is bored. We would play games like 'UNO' or backgammon. I even taught him how to play blackjack. I found out that this was a good way to learn and teach him math.

The last shocking story!

Some days I would ask him if he would like to talk to his mom. I would dial the number and hand him the phone and walk out of the room so he could have his privacy.

Five minutes later he would tell me that he is finished talking to her. Astonished, I would see if she was still on the phone. "He didn't have much to say," she would tell me. "He said that he wanted to talk you. I guess he just wanted to hear your voice," I would reply.

I want to show you how thoughtful 'Levern' is. One day we talked about all of us going to Germany to visit. Since 'Levern' had never been to Germany, I thought that it would be a good idea if the Bo visits his mom while 'Levern' and I vacationed in another part of Germany.

After checking the airline fares and the hotel prices we could not afford it at that time. This is when 'Levern' came up with the most unselfish and unbeliev-able idea. 'Levern' suggested that we could pay for my ex who wasn't working to come to the states and that we could put her up in Base Lodging. 'Levern' said that the Bo could spend as much time with her, show his mom his room, school and meet some of his friends. I could not believe she would want to spend any money to do anything for my ex. That's love! That's real love!

I called my ex wife the following weekend to give her the news. I let the Bo talk to her first. As usual, the conversation went rather quickly. He gave me the phone. I told her what 'Levern' suggested and I told her that it was a good idea.

My ex wife listened to me. She told me that it was very nice of 'Levern' to come up with such a great suggestion to visit the Bo. Then out of nowhere she asked me if I had ever taken the DNA test.

You may remember in Chapter 30, my ex wife and I had one last argument. This argument centered on me taking a DNA test to prove that I was not the father of her second child. That DNA test would have cost me 1,000 dollars. How many times have I written in this book, that we only had unprotected sex once?

Well, my ex wife brought up that subject again. By now, I surely thought that she had gotten the message. It had been at least 4 months since we talked on that topic and I thought to my self 'if you had not received any official blood work through the mail, guess what? You are not getting any?"

I was preparing for another huge argument!

Before I could answer her question, she dropped the biggest **bombshell** on me.

She said that she couldn't make the trip because she was pregnant (again) with her third child!!!

I did not have anything thing to say.

She told me the first few weeks after I deployed to Kosovo, the African guy and her were 'messing' around for a few months. He lived at her place for a while. Then he moved out. She said they still liked each other and he would visit her from time to time. Their relationship was not serious.

One day, they got into an argument (what else is new?). That night, her room-mate stayed at home and watched the Bo. She went to a club down the street and met another African! (Let's call him #2.) After the club she and #2 went back to her apartment. They had a one-night stand. The next day, (get this) she felt guilty that she had a one-night stand with #2 and told him it was a mistake.

After #2 left her house, she called #1 on the phone and apologized for their argument they had the previous day. They made up and all was well. During the entire time she was with #1, she never told him about her brief encounter with #2.

A couple of days later #1 moved back in her apartment and all was normal. Or so she thought.

A few months went by, when she asked me about getting the DNA test. She heard me explode and told her no. The same day she also asked #1 to get a DNA test as well.

I asked her how she could afford the DNA test. She told me that the German government charged her portion of her 'kindergeld' account.

My ex wife told me at first #1 hesitated but finally after a month, he took the test. She (and him) found out that her second child was not #1's child!

She had #2's phone number and convinced him to take a DNA test. He agreed and the test proved that it was indeed #2's child. She never heard from him again and she thinks that he went back to Africa because he traveled to the country illegally.

She told me that #1 was not happy with her at all. They had another argument and he moved out again. Believe it or not, a few days later he moved back in with her and have reconciled. Now she is having **his** baby. Whatever…

As if this does not get any stranger than this, she told me that both African's knew each other. I guess there is a small African community in Stuttgart.

So, I figured out that throughout my deployment, she had toyed with my emotions. For an example:

In chapter eight, she voiced 'concern' over my deployment. This led me to believe that she really cared for me.

In chapter twelve, she sounded enthusiastic and offered a glimmer of hope. She mentioned that she couldn't move all of the furniture back into my apartment by herself.

In chapter fourteen, she gets pregnant, by whom?

In chapter eighteen, she was showing the first signs of confusion. Arguing with me over petty stuff, or was she really auguring through me at #1?

In chapter twenty-one, when I saw her she looked lost. Did she have doubts as to who baby it was?

The bottom line in all this, I had been played.

I am *so* glad that I got out of that relationship!

'A new love'

With all of the art that I bought, I learned how to frame. 'Levern' was so supportive in my newfound hobby. As I have mentioned, I fell in love with the art of Charles Bibbs, C'Babi Bayoc, Justin Bua, and Don Stivers! I was buying art at a fast pace and quickly ran out of wall space.

I heard through a friend of mine that Mr. Bibbs was coming to a Seattle art gallery in a few months. I was so excited. I was going to meet the man that I admired.

Unbeknownst to me I also had in my possession four compact discs with his art on them. I found his official Internet site and emailed him. I told him how much of a fan I was of his. I asked if he would sign my CDs along with some of my unframed art when he came to Seattle. His wife emailed me and said that it would be his pleasure to do it for me. Man that made my day!

One day, I saw a CD in the Post Exchange's music section. The art on the front cover caught my eyes. I noticed this CD was by the R and B artist, Prince. I purchased it right away. This was the first time that I bought a CD because of the art illustration.

When I got home, I thumbed through the booklet on the inside of the CD. At the very bottom on the last page was the liner note that read 'Art Illustration by C'Babi.' The next day I searched the Internet for the name of C'Babi. I found his official site with a phone number.

This time (for some reason), I decided to call instead of sending an email. When the voice on the other end picked up, I thought that it was one of his assistants. I told him that I liked C'Babi's art and wanted to purchase the print of the *Rainbow Children*. I was sad to hear that it was unavailable. Prince bought the rights to it and could not be sold.

Then the voice on the other end of the phone thanked me for appreciating *his* art. I was shocked to learn that I was talking to C'Babi himself! After a long conversation, I talked him into doing a commissioned piece of my family. It turned out great!

I made two videotapes. I sent one to my ex wife and the other I sent to my mother. I waited a few days to call my mother. I wanted to see if she got the videotape. She fell in love with what she saw and she was very proud of me. Then she gave me the shock of my life when she told me that she was dating again.

I knew something was up. My father had been dead for almost six years. Whenever I called she told me that she was doing ok but she was also sick with this or ailing with that. The last few times we talked; she never mentioned about begin sick. It's funny that when you are in love all, that 'sickness' goes away!

She knew her new friend for many years. They went to school back when they were teenagers. He liked her but could never get close to her because as she puts it, 'she had all the boys looking at her'.

Her voice sounded so happy but a little apprehensive. She really liked him but she was still holding on to the past. My father treated her so badly for years that my mom was a little afraid to step in to another relationship that looked and sounded great.

She told me that her new friend has been a lawyer for over forty years. He has been an established member of the community. He has more court cases than he knows what to do with.

His first wife died a few years ago, so they were a natural fit. I could tell she really liked him. She went on about him for over twenty minutes. I was happy for her. Now in the winter years of her life she had found happiness and I too had found it as well. What a way to end this book on such a happy note. Everyone was doing so well.

'Déjà vu all over again'

There was a problem at work however. There were rumblings about sending a solider on a deployment to Bosnia for six months. The solider had to be a supply sergeant that was a Sergeant First Class (E-7). In the brigade I was working in, there were only three Sergeants First Class.

There was an E-7 that was already in Kosovo. There was another E-7 that was due to leave to go to Korea in a year. Then there was me. I had been out of the Balkans for about thirteen months, but only been at Ft. Lewis for only six months.

I was hoping that they would send the guy that was heading to Korea instead of me. The soldier told me that he had never been on a deployment. I just knew they were going to pick him.

There were meetings. There were discussions. Finally there was a decision to send the other solider to the Balkans! Man I was lucky!

I told 'Levern' and she was happy that I was not going to be deployed. We went on with our lives.

Until….

The E-7 left to go to Bosnia. First he had to stop at Fort Benning, Ga. It is there where the army gives you equipment, training and all the health and dental check ups before you deploy to any part of the world.

He arrived on a Sunday and by Tuesday we heard that he was having medical problems. He had an irregular heartbeat. At work we received emails about his health. We were told that they would keep him a few more days there to monitor his heart rate. The next day he came back to Fort Lewis. You know what that meant for me, another deployment. Déjà vu.

Let me say that my unit did try its best not to send me. Fort Lewis Headquarters needed my unit to fill this slot so with many apologies I got 'stuck'.

I was told that I had two weeks to prepare. I told 'Levern'. She took it rather calmly but my mother had difficulty in taking the news. She cried when I told her that I would be leaving on another deployment.

The Bo took the news in stride (as usual). He said ok and told me that he would miss me.

I was upset that I had to leave. Everything was just about settled in our lives. I guess that I acted a little unselfish about getting deployed again. After all, I was married for 5 weeks and I am deploying again.

Kosovo was a yearlong tour. After that the move from Germany to the states was a bit for me as a single parent. Then I moved from Lakewood to my house on post. I went through a divorce and just got remarried and now I was ready for a 'break' when this happens. It shows you that in today's world you have to live everyday to the fullest.

The two weeks flew by. I sat down and wrote out all the bills that had to be paid. I wrote six months of checks and put them in corresponding envelopes. 'Levern' took a crash course with all of my outstanding payments. This task was a bit daunting, but 'Levern' caught on quickly. We went for a drive around Fort Lewis. I showed her some short cuts around post. I showed her the medical and dental facility. I updated emergency names and numbers.

A week before I left, Charles Bibbs came to the Kenneth Behm Gallery. I brought my compact discs, my camera and a couple of unframed art for Charles to sign. I purchased yet another piece of his art entitled, *The Music Maker II*.

My bags were packed and on Sunday July 14th 2002, I left to go to Fort Benning GA. 'Levern' drove me to the airport. I went over the things that I covered at home; when 'Levern' broke in and told me no need to worry everything will be fine. Man, I got a good woman!

And so it goes life in the army, on another deployment. Damn.

Epilogue

The last time I had written notes for this book was at least four years ago. Allow me to give you some updates:

- 'Levern' and I are still very much married and in love.

- I still have custody of the Bo. He is doing great in school, and now 12 years old. We still have not made it to Germany, nor has my ex wife made it to the states. He still talks to her at least once a month. Maybe next year we will go to Germany.

- I still speak to my ex wife parents at least four times a year.

- My eldest child graduated from Old Dominion University.

- My ex wife still does not have a job and is taking care of her two kids all by herself. She is not dating anyone. African #1 was also in the country illegally and thus was deported.

- I have not received any money from my ex wife. From time to time she sends the Bo 'kiddie' items from Germany.

- I saw CPT Jung (now Major) in the mess last year (in all places) at Djibouti, Africa. It had been at least 5 years since we last seen each other in Kosovo.

- I still email my pen pal monthly. We are still in contact with each other for 6 years now.

- The clock that the two boys gave me in Kosovo, hangs in the Bo's room.

- As for me, the deployments did not stop. Soon after I came back from a 7 month tour of Bosnia, I have been to:
  Camp Hovey, Korea (near the DMZ). A year without my family.
  Mac Dill AFB in Tampa, FL where I have been deployed to:
  Doha, Qatar
  Djibouti, Africa
  Bagram, Afghanistan

- In July 2006, my retirement from the army was approved. I will retire in 2007. At the rank of Master Sergeant (E-8).

My mom's love interest did not pan out. It fizzled after five months. She was really afraid of getting into another relationship. My father must have really done some damage to her. She really never trusted another man again.

She died on August 5 2006. You may remember I sent her chapters from this book. After she died, I was going through some of her belongings. I found a shoe box that was taped together. In it, were the chapters that I sent to her along with some photos of me.

My regret is that she never saw this book in print.

I love you Mom!!!!

978-0-595-41609-7
0-595-41609-8